MW01104252

To my new friend John

The Market Entry Toolkit

The Market Entry Toolkit
by Bill Decker

The Market Entry Toolkit

by

Bill Decker

Contents

How to Use This Book

This toolkit is organized intuitively and divided into sections. No, we can't teach all you need to possibly know about how to pick foreign markets and how to correctly enter them with just this toolkit. But we can get you familiar with the issues involved and more knowledgeable about the processes and decisions that have to be made.

INTRODUCTION

THE BUSINESS ISSUES CHECKLIST

An Inventory of Business Concerns Abroad

This section is meant to acquaint the reader with many of the business issues your firm will encounter when considering and choosing foreign markets. It is a checklist of many of the pitfalls and obstacles abroad. It should serve as a good basis of discussion when considering strategies in International Business.

LESSONS FROM THE ROAD: GLOBAL BUSINESS 1 - LINERS

This next section is filled with one-liners and anecdotes about International Business.

AUDIO: HOW TO LOSE YOUR SHIRT ABROAD

This audio program (brought to you by The Lemonade

Stand) presents an overview of the various ways your firm can be taken advantage of in foreign markets. It's a classic "how not to" guide and we sprinkle in plenty of humor. This has aired in several places in the USA and abroad and is an entertaining introduction to the difficulties involved in International Business. This section can be found at our website: http://marketentrytoolkit.com/welcome/readers/.

MARKET ENTRY PATHWAYS

This white paper defines the various modes of entry into foreign markets, discusses the pros and cons of each and is laced with many helpful examples.

MY ARCHIVE OF "HOW TO" ARTICLES FROM THE DENVER BUSINESS JOURNAL

These articles were published between 2005 and 2011 and contain "how to" strategies for companies engaged in global business. Most of this course will discuss market entry strategies. However, these articles include pieces on outsourcing, negotiation, licensing, branding, culture and managing foreign nationals.

INTRODUCTION TO THE MARKET ACCESS SCREEN

This is a quick intro to describe the Market Access Screen and how it can help your firm. The audio can be found at http://marketentrytoolkit.com/welcome/readers/ .

THE MARKET ACCESS SCREEN

This is a proprietary tool built to help firms compare overseas markets using some real criteria. This grading system will help a firm use objective data to examine the pros and cons of different markets. At the end of the exercise, users will have a raw score that they can use to back up their decisions. The Market Access Screen is a living document; one must be able to manipulate and modify it. It is available to you for free under "additional resources" below. The Market Access Screen was created after engaging in hundreds of international market entry deals abroad.

AUDIO: HOW TO USE THE MARKET ACCESS SCREEN

This is an audio program explaining how to use the included Market Access Screen. Though the Market Access Screen is self-explanatory, there may be a few terms and concepts that need further definition. You'll notice that the various sound bytes are in order and numbered, starting with number 11. Again this is found on our website.

THE LICENSING CHECKLIST

Licensing your product or technology can often be the most profitable way into a foreign market. This checklist discusses all the points a firm needs to consider doing technology transfer or licensing deals abroad.

WHAT SHOULD BE IN ANY MARKETING PLAN

By now you've become familiar with the issues involved. You have received some education on processes to select a market and become aware of the pitfalls that await you. It is time to build a market entry plan. The outline in this section is a good way to organize the contents (and your thoughts) for that plan.

CONCLUSION

ADDITIONAL RESOURCES

To download and use the Market Access Screen, please visit

www.marketaccessscreen.com

INTRODUCTION

How does a firm actually select a foreign market? How does a company figure out which overseas markets to sell its products? How does a company make an informed decision? What methodology can you use to make the process easier?

In 30 years of international market entry experience I've seen firms pick markets for the craziest reasons. I've seen CEOs choose France as a market because they want to go see the Eiffel tower! I've seen company boards pick England because "they speak English over there." I've seen people read an article about China and then decide to launch their company in that market.

After traveling the globe for decades and seeing every possible mistake made (and making quite a few myself) I decided to develop a cohesive methodology for selecting and entering a foreign market – the Market Entry Toolkit.

I knew that a successful Market Entry Toolkit would have to provide a company with the tools to logically and systematically compare one market to another while allowing the company flexibility to modify its analysis for a customized solution.

The Market Entry Toolkit has to be very robust. Variables such as market size, culture, infrastructure, ability to exchange money freely and other factors must all be taken into account. The Market Entry Toolkit also has to consider the cultural fit regarding a firm, its products or services and the marketplace it is attempting to reach. At the same time, simplicity is important so the methodology can be communicated to CEOs, CFOs, Boards of Directors, sales people, staff and customers alike.

The Market Entry Toolkit is the result of thirty years of market entry experience involving hundreds of different deals and clients all over the world. I've worked in many markets while living on 4 continents.

The Market Entry Toolkit starts by acquainting the user with basic issues involved in overseas business. The Market Entry Toolkit then provides tips and pointers in an easy to digest one-liner form.

The Market Entry Toolkit then provides the primary methodology and framework to choose a foreign market – the "market access screen" – which takes the user step by step through the process and analysis.

You will also receive an outline of what an international marketing plan should contain, so that you can effectively build one yourself, once you have chosen the right foreign market for your firm.

The information you need is provided through audio, video, articles, podcasts, white papers and other media. As an example, the Market Entry Toolkit contains an audio program, with humor blended in, explaining "how to lose your shirt abroad" (the pitfalls of international business).

The user of this toolkit will also see dozens of articles; each one is relevant to a specific area of international business.

The Market Entry Toolkit is no substitute for good old-fashioned strategic planning, but hopefully it will bring insight, guidance and tools to firms wishing to expand overseas or needing to support the rationale for their existing decisions and direction.

Any tool is only as good as the person who is using it. Therefore, the Market Entry Toolkit will help educate users so that they can be more effective as they work to plan and enter foreign markets.

As International Business becomes a necessary part of our global economy, more and more consultants are entering the arena. Some of the consultants out there are good and some are simply frauds. The Market Entry Toolkit contains information helpful to find and evaluate expertise.

Once you've had a chance to use the Market Entry Toolkit, feel free to contact us for a telephone consultation.

And drop us a line to let us know how we can improve the toolkit.

Enjoy the journey,

Bill Decker

www.partnersinternational.com

Business Issues Checklist

This is a listing of many (not all) of the business concerns a firm will encounter when trying to gain markets abroad. Your industry may also have special issues and obstacles to consider.

MARKET RESEARCH: IDENTIFYING AND LOCATING BUYERS/ COMPETITORS/ MARKET FORCES

Are connections necessary in this market and if so, is your firm connected in the market? Can you purchase these connections?

What is the size of the potential market and is there an expressed market need?

What language does the market speak? Are there several languages or dialects? Do you have people who can communicate with them?

What are some of the available sources of information on potential buyers, written and personal, public and private?

How does one assess the reliability of the information and the source?

Is the market organized, can you find information? Where are the written sources located and how can they be obtained?

How difficult is it to obtain non-sensitive "inside" information about a company?

How might an organization which is a potential buyer be structured? What is the typical hierarchy and where is the power likely to lie?

Where in the organization will the decision be made to buy or not to buy your product or service?

If the decision will be made by a single person, what is the probable title and what responsibilities would that person have?

If the decision is likely to be made by a group or committee, describe it. Is one function (i.e. Engineering, Finance, etc.) likely to wield the real power?

What are the relevant issues regarding protocol when approaching a potential customer?

What is the best Mode of Entry into this market, and are you comfortable with it? (E.g. licensing, co-production, co-branding, direct export).

ADVERTISING

Is there an image of business, in general, that is expected? Is there an image of the particular industry that is expected?

What characteristics do potential customers look for in a vendor? What characterizes a tarnished business image–one that would not make it through the front door?

What is the attitude in general toward the USA and American products and services?

What is the attitude toward advertising? Is it an acceptable means of company and brand promotion?

In some countries marketers marshal an array of advertising media and techniques to secure public awareness of their companies and products. Are those same devices accepted in the country under consideration? Are there any distinctive differences in that regard?

Is there a point at which the amount of advertising becomes offensive, or so ostentatious that it is self-defeating?

Are there any cultural taboos regarding which media are used or, particularly, about message content, including choice of words, colors, and graphics?

Are there advertising/promotional media that are considered essential for the participant's particular industry? (For example, if a European publisher is not represented at the Frankfurt Book Fair it loses prestige, reputation and, presumably, orders).

Can you re-purpose any existing advertising?

Do you need local advertising, websites, business cards, or addresses?

NETWORKING AND CONTACTS

Are introductions essential?

Are there ways to meet key people in non-business settings that are more effective or acceptable than other means?

What are expected networking methods? What are accepted means of developing acquaintances and friendships among potential customers?

What is the attitude toward mixing business with pleasure? What is the usual behavior in this regard?

Is business entertaining by vendors desirable, expected or resisted? Is there a point before which a vendor should not extend such an invitation in order to avoid risking a negative impression?

If business entertaining is acceptable, where is entertaining expected to be done? (At home, in restaurants, at the theater, at sporting events, or elsewhere)?

Is club membership important in meeting key business people? How easy is it to obtain such memberships? Is being an expatriate an advantage or disadvantage in obtaining club membership?

How involved does your family need to be?

Are there any cultural taboos regarding your gender?

SALES

Does this market require local sales talent?

In face-to-face meetings, are there any cultural conventions that the American sales person should observe?

Is the sales person held to a different ethical standard than is the population in general?

What are the possible negative consequences if conventions or standards are overlooked?

What traits or qualities are considered admirable for a sales person to display?

What behavior is considered to be offensive?

Sales people in any culture must be assertive to a degree. At what point does assertiveness become interpreted as aggressiveness in this culture?

Are there specific selling techniques in this industry that are particularly effective in this culture?

How important is call preparation? How would a typical business person react to a sales representative who spent significant time during a face-to-face meeting asking basic questions about the company's products, markets, etc.?

Is it necessary to work with administrative assistants? If so, what are some acceptable ways of winning over the administrative assistant or secretary who can block the sales representative's access to a key decision maker?

How widespread is the use of American English in commerce?

How serious is a lack of fluency in the customer's language or dialect?

Is there any significant benefit to speaking the customer's tongue?

American business conversation is liberally sprinkled with sports metaphors.

What metaphors are commonly used in the culture under consideration?

THE PURCHASE DECISION

Is this an individual or collective decision?

Is the time taken to close a sale proportional to the value, size and complexity of the sale? Are negotiations conducted expeditiously or is the tempo slower, with the negotiations more formal and choreographed than in the U.S.?

What behavior might be interpreted as "American impatience," and what would the reaction be?

What might be telltale verbal or nonverbal signs of indifference or hostility?

What are the key criteria leading to the first repeat orders?

What priority might be assigned to?

- Reputation of the vendor

- Perceived quality of the product/service

- Perseverance

- Dependability of the vendor, e.g. timely delivery

- Kickbacks, bribes

- Personal qualities of the company representative: personality

  » Trustworthiness

  » Responsiveness to requests, complaints

> » Other

- Customer intimacy?

Are there any unique aspects of the country's commercial code that will affect the Document of Sale?

Are contracts used?

What are the standard provisions in sales contracts?

CUSTOMER RELATIONS

Other than consistent timely delivery of quality products or services, what are acceptable means of maintaining good customer relations?

Gifts? Personal gifts or with a business logo? When?

How do you balance gift exchanges with your personal and company ethics?

Entertainment? What kind?

Favors asked by the client?

Extended time spent together?

What kind of relationship does your customer expect to develop with you?

How is this relationship built and maintained?

What does the customer most value in this relationship?

What are the limits of the relationship?

How frequent is on-going customer/vendor contact for the purpose of maintaining the relationship?

How much information of a proprietary nature does your customer expect and want?

LOGISTICS

Can you get money in and out of the market?

Do you need to sell directly or through intermediaries?

Is the government a barrier or an aide to your progress?

Can you travel to the market easily?

Are the amenities necessary for you to conduct business available?

Are offsets or investments required?

Are there quotas on your product?

Is your product being sold into a protected industry?

Are their prohibitive tariffs?

How will you handle disputes? Is this a pay-in-advance country? If not, are the players creditworthy?

Do you need a local partner?

Will in country production be demanded?

Are licenses easy or difficult to obtain?

Is E-commerce practical in this market?

NEGOTIATION STYLES

Are negotiations structured or loose?

How long do negotiations take in this market?

Can your firm invest enough resources to negotiate properly?

Are negotiations firm, or do they continue throughout the life of the relationship?

LESSONS FROM THE ROAD: GLOBAL BUSINESS 1-LINERS

This next section contains lessons from the road learned through decades of international marketing, management and negotiation. The road spanned 62 countries on 5 continents. The chapter is broken into easy to digest 1-liners in business. It will increase your mileage and point out those avenues needed for growth.

INTERNATIONAL PROVERBS TO QUOTE AND THINK ABOUT

A wise person hears one word, but understands two.

—The Talmud

How a society treats its lowest members is a measure of its merit.

—Scandinavian proverb

If you are going to tell the truth, have one foot in the stirrup.

—Turkish proverb

The fat pig gets slaughtered.

—Chinese proverb

The tall blade of grass gets cut down.

—Socialized countries' expression

In Russia, a real man does not negotiate.

—Russian rule of thumb

It is not what you know, it is who.

—Everyone, much truer internationally

We can always fool a foreigner.

—Chinese proverb

When someone has no family, he is considered unlucky.

—Southeast Asian proverb

The nail sticking up gets hammered down.

—Japanese proverb

Love is the food of life, but travel is the dessert.

—Singaporean proverb

We don't care about the package; we care what is IN the package.

—Dutch proverb

If you don't shoot, you always miss.

—Dutch proverb

Observe, then imitate.

—Japanese motto

In Europe, white men go into rooms and decide how markets will be divided. In Asia, the market decides for itself.

—Nihon Kezai Shinbun

(Japanese Economic Journal)

Necessity is the mother of invention, desperation is the father. But assumption is the brother of all screw-ups.

—John Kuranz

In times of great trouble, you are allowed to walk with the Devil... but only until you have crossed the bridge.

—Bulgarian proverb

When I am weak, how can I negotiate with you? When I am strong, why should I?

—Arab proverb

After we have clothes on our backs and food on our tables, then we worry about ethics.

—Chinese proverb

A small boat turns back faster.

—Asian proverb

Look around the corner, see what is there.

—Israeli proverb

Business is managing mentalities.

—French proverb

To travel effectively one needs only two things: patience and a willingness to learn.

—Confucius

Outsourcing is no substitute for innovating at home.

—Unknown (American)

We are slaves to our history.

—Greek proverb

If you are connected, you can get in.

—German proverb

Americans are superficial.

—Every European I've ever met

Americans are the only people in the world who do business with strangers.

—Bill Decker

GENDER ISSUES

In the USA "women in business" is surrounded with change, excitement and controversy. In the USA we like to discuss our controversial issues. We even put our problems on television!

Most cultures are vastly different about discussing their changes in thinking and their changes in culture. "It's a man's world" can hold true to a greater extent overseas than in the USA. Women in global business (often) face unfair challenges, such as:

- In Asia, women often are not present at business functions.

- It is difficult for many cultures to fathom that a man can be subordinate to a woman in business.

- Many men are completely unfamiliar with women in business altogether.

- You will usually be negotiating with men when you are abroad...and only men in the Arab world and most of Asia.

- Many languages have a masculine and a feminine form. The feminine form is often more indirect.

- When a businessman travels with a businesswoman, many only see a businessman.

- When you discuss what is "politically correct," you might ask: "whose politics?" Derogatory remarks may be more cultural than personal.

  » Example: "In your country you treat the women as citizens. In ours, we treat them like women." —Greek expression

- Ms. is usually Ms. understood.

CULTURAL AWARENESS AND UNDERSTANDING

- The single biggest difference in cultures is the perception of "time."

  » Example: the English language has words to express time that no other culture has: personal time, overtime, spend time, waste time, borrowed time, double time, time is money, and time-and-a half.

- Get a cultural guide wherever you go: Someone who has "been there, done that."

- If there is no relationship, assume no trust.

- The sense of shame (losing face) can be a matter of life of death.

  » Example: my Karate instructor used to compete in death tournaments. When asked what would happen if he lost, his answer was that he would rather lose than face his family and friends.

- Make sure you have an "Uncle."

  » Example: when an Asian boy disagrees with his father, he cannot confront him. He uses his uncle to intercede. This way, there is no loss of face. This model applies for business in Asia as well.

- When Asians are embarrassed, they laugh.

- A friend is someone you will lie for.

- Chinese will greet each other by asking: "Have you eaten yet?"

- The USA is the only country in the world that refers to a national sporting championship as "The World Series."

- Americans see history as in the past. Europeans feel they are part of history.

- "Rude" and "Polite" are cultural.

- Many people you interact with may look, dress and speak like you. The similarity ends there.

- In Europe, coffee means hello. In Asia, it's tea. In the third world, it's food.

- Show me a country's eating habits, and I'll show you its culture.

  » Example: Americans and Northern Europeans have a concept of "my food." Elsewhere, food is shared, often eaten from common plates.

- Never expect them to hear what you hear, see what you see, know what you know, or assume what you assume.

- Every country has its hierarchies.

- Example: in Asia, the older you are, the more respect you deserve. Nodding may mean: "I've heard you," not "I agree with you."

- "Unethical" does not exist.

- Ethics are a suit of clothes...yours are different than mine.

- Never thank a Central or Eastern European for "their time." It will make their colleagues suspicious.

- Many cultures have difficulties putting things in writing.

- Politics, Religion, Sex and Business. Americans like to separate these ideas; the rest of the planet groups them together.

  » Example: many countries stamp their citizens' passports with their religious classifications.

- » Example: you may be asked about your marital status and political beliefs. In many parts of the world, religion will surely be a topic.

- Power distance is the perception of a leader's importance.

  - » Example: the USA has low power distance. We call our leader "Mister," and joke about him every day. Iran has the highest power distance. They call their leader Ayatollah (reflection of God).

- Content cultures concentrate on exactly what was said or done. Context cultures focus on who said or did it, and under what circumstances.

  - » Example: you can always spot the highest- ranking person at a Japanese (context culture) meeting...he is sitting farthest from the door.

- Independent cultures admire entrepreneurs and loners.

- Collective cultures look at groups for identity.

  - » Example: Koreans advertise cigarettes by showing groups of men smoking. In the USA, we have the Marlboro man: alone, tough and fearless.

- Task Specific cultures judge the value proposition offered.

- Relationship Specific cultures value the quality of the relationships. They have fewer friends, and greater loyalty to them.

  » Example: cold-calling is an American phenomenon. It doesn't really exist elsewhere, as almost all other cultures are relationship specific.

- Mono-chronic cultures do one thing at a time.

- Poly-chronic cultures do several things at once.

- The difference between public and private varies from culture to culture.

  » Example: many Northern Europeans use their first initial on business correspondence, so you cannot determine the gender of the author. It is private and irrelevant.

- Business is done by introduction, and most cultures are very careful about giving them.

  » Example: in an extreme case, I was walking in Madrid with a Spaniard. We ran into a friend of his. He stopped and spoke with his friend for 5 minutes, without introducing us. This was natural to both Spaniards.

- The system is more important than the people.

PLANNING

- The first question is: "WHY?" WHY are you doing business there, WHY have you chosen your mode of entry and most importantly, WHY will they work with you?

- When entering a foreign market, you must ask: "How much are you willing to lose?"

- Use the "double-double" rule...it will cost twice as much and take twice as long.

- You can't do international deals without educating your deal makers on how it's done overseas.

- Determine your own moral line, even if you do not express it.

- Figure out what you mean by "Western," "Central," and "Eastern" Europe before using those terms.

- Americans usually make their business trips too short.

- Never make assumptions about security.

- Having an employee who speaks French does not mean you have an employee who can do business with France.

- In countries you visit, look for context umbrellas. Perception is often limited to what realities exist under them.

- Remember, there is no such thing as "the international market."

LANGUAGE (TRANSLATING/INTERPRETATION)

- If you want to sell me something, you had better do it in my language.

- Language is the single biggest cultural barrier.

- Humor rarely translates.

- "American" is not the international business language. American euphemisms like "pass the buck" and "off the wall" have no meaning abroad.

- Many Asian cultures have no words for "yes" and "no."

- Someone who speaks English and Thai is not necessarily a translator.

- Translate, and then "back translate" (into the initial language).

- Always use your own interpreter, not theirs.

- Pick a title that can be translated. The same is true for a product name.

- Translate your business card.

SALES AND MARKETING

- U.S. firms will start the marketing process by asking: "What problem is solved by our product?" Overseas firms will start by figuring out who they know in a given market.

- Many American companies worry about their competitors. Asian companies worry about their customers.

- Most companies will work with their established vendors to fix problems. Americans will switch vendors more quickly.

» Example: a British firm bidding for a project in Japan found that the client revealed their bid to a local (Japanese) competitor.

- Assume everyone knows everyone...especially in your industry.

  » Extreme example: in business school, a colleague from New Delhi once told me that if a student from India were to arrive at our program, there would be a 90% chance that he knows him or his family. The professional community is very small in India.

- When Asian business isn't done man-to-man, it is done family-to-family.

- Getting a permit to build a store in Malaysia does not mean you can open your shop. Shops exist on streets, in cities, not on federal land.

- A European food distributor once asked me: "If we carry your product, what will happen to the products already on the shelves?"

- Many European governments need high European product content in their purchases.

- In South America, Europe, Asia, Africa and the Middle East, you will be dealing with governments.

- You may know your industry and all about your company. Do you know your target market? One question I always ask: "How often do you take your distributors to dinner?"

- In Central and Eastern Europe, the secret was never selling; the secret was always buying. Beware of de-facto partnerships. If "everyone knows" you are negotiating with a certain company, it will be assumed you are partners.

- When picking partners remember you often get only one chance. A failed deal can close the market forever. Take your time. After all, would you rush into a marriage?

NEGOTIATING

- Many cultures believe a contract comes first and then negotiations begin.

- Silence does not imply consent.

- You will often negotiate with groups.

- Consensus is important in socialized countries.

- Japanese work out all of the potential problems first, and then make a deal; Americans do the opposite.

- In meetings, everyone seems to look at the person with the calculator.

- Learn a few words of their language, at least enough to apologize for not speaking it.

- "Face" is crucial in Asia. Humiliation can cost you your business, and often much more.

  » Example: even when dating, Asian men will often ask

a woman for a date through an intermediary. Thus, there is no loss of face if she declines. She will decline via the messenger.

- Try to ask: "What does success in your market look like?" It will be a direct question, but one easily answered.

- Many countries consider a handshake to be a commitment.

- Americans and Western Europeans are said to "say what they mean, and mean what they say." With other cultures, this is often not the case.

- Expect to eat when you discuss business.

- Learn to draw pictures and charts to demonstrate your points. (Upside down)

- Communication is not what I say; it is what you hear.

MANAGING STAFF FROM OTHER COUNTRIES

- A U.S. firm located in Germany is neither an American firm nor a German firm; it is a very different hybrid.

- Use paternalism instead of confrontation to motivate employees.

- Have foreign employees write a synopsis of what they have been assigned to do.

- American managers look for additional skill sets; European managers look for employees that will "fit in."

- Jobs may be more important than profit.

- » Example: in Poland, small towns look at plant managers as "employers." How will you motivate the managers to lay off staff?

- Europeans and Asians will often reward loyalty rather than merit.

  - » Example: Asians will often advance within companies because they show blind obedience to superiors.

- The myth of working at one company for life still exists.

- Often, HR can't fire foreign workers.

  - » Example: many employers in Europe commit to paying 50-70% of an employee's salary after termination. You may be stuck paying employees until they find another job! Did you ever wonder why there are locals in the pubs all day in Europe?

- You will work Saturdays in Asia.

- In the third world, one must pay local wages.

  - » Example: in a factory in Central America, we were paying twice the local wage. The workers would get their pay, take an additional month off (without telling us) and return one month later expecting their jobs back!

- Chinese bosses are said to have a "velvet fist."

- Europeans cannot work together until they have discussed the war. (WWII)

LEGAL

- The relationship is more important than the governing laws.

  » Example: if you manufacture in Asia and your first shipment is defective, it means you must work on the relationship.

- In many overseas cases, a lawyer's presence can mean: "I don't trust you." If you need to bring attorneys have camouflage business cards printed.

- When a product injures a consumer, an American will hire an attorney to obtain satisfaction. Europeans will go to their government.

- Overseas you have absolutely no rights. You are a guest...often an unwelcome one.

- "Overtime" can be illegal.

- There is no debt on Chinese balance sheets; debts are personal.

- Polish tax inspectors receive commissions on what they find.

- There is no such thing as "international law."

QUESTIONS TO ASK YOURSELF

- How do you know when you are "in?"

- Is this the Brazilian way of telling me that you don't want to do this? (Pick any nationality)

- Do they respect my authority?

- I know our way of doing this, but what is their way?

- Have I heard this correctly?

- What assumptions might be underlying their actions?

- How can I relate to the people in this country; what steps can I take to do so?

- Who does my "employee" work for?

- How do these people handle food? Is there a way to understand the culture from it?

TRAVELER'S TIPS

- When you visit, read about their geography, politics, economy, culture and demographics.

- Learn some French. It's considered the language of diplomacy. And it's in your passport.

- Buy USD $100 worth of their currency before you leave.

- Don't spare the expense. Get the right luggage.

- When in doubt, drink boiled water. Or tea.

- Never travel with more than you can carry.

- If you have "food issues" stay home!

- Don't get offended.

- Be prepared for the whole world to have a cigarette in its mouth.

- You are an ambassador. Be prepared to discuss U.S. policy and politics.

- Remember "the Golden Rule." He who has the gold, rules.

LESSONS LEARNED IN THE TRENCHES

- Americans are the only people in the world who do business with strangers.

- When the logical arguments stop making sense, you must look for the illogical ones.

- If you have a Russian problem, you must have a Russian solution.

- When in Rome, do as the Romans. (Don't try to actually be Roman)

- Success at home doesn't imply success abroad.

AUDIO: HOW TO LOSE YOUR SHIRT ABROAD

Go to: http://marketentrytoolkit.com/welcome/readers/ to listen to the following audio links:

1) INTERNATIONAL ASSUMPTIONS

2) INTERNATIONAL ASSUMPTIONS PART 2

3) OVERSEAS MISUNDERSTANDINGS

4) NUMBER 1 OVERSEAS MISUNDERSTANDING

5) INTERNATIONAL POLICIES AND PROCEDURES

6) INTERNATIONAL POLICIES AND PROCEDURES, PART 2

7) DISHONESTY ABROAD

8) DISHONESTY ABROAD, PART 2

Market Entry Pathways
Modes of Entry, Explanation and Processes

The business world of today calls for expanding sales and profits in order to achieve ever-increasing earnings. Business owners and managers must look for any available opportunities to keep their market share and expand into new markets. What happens when their local market becomes saturated? The savvy leader is inclined to search abroad for any and all potential new markets for their product or service. New markets offer the possibility of increasing total revenue and/or decreasing the costs of goods sold, thereby increasing profits. Entering new markets may also allow a company to follow its existing customers abroad, attack competitors in their home markets, guarantee a continued supply of raw materials, acquire technology or ingenuity, diversify geographically, or satisfy the stockholders' desire to expand.

In many cases, with many companies, it is survival. There simply isn't enough domestic demand to keep many firms in business, without going overseas.

Once management has made the decision to expand and has determined the target market or markets, the next question is obviously "how". Selecting a mode for entering or expanding in a foreign market is one of the most crucial strategic decisions that can be made by a company. Weighing all factors and choosing the proper mode of entry can result in huge competitive advantages, while making a poor decision can lead to the demise of the company.

43

Often, international people without the knowledge base or the necessary contacts are tasked with "going international." 90% of the time, they will fail.

Foreign market penetration can be done by a variety of different methods; each possibility should be assessed before the process begins.

Following is a comprehensive list of various modes of entry that can be utilized when entering or expanding in a foreign market.

1. ACQUISITIONS:

Purchasing an existing company.

PROS:

- Established market
- Skilled workers available (often not found through normal employee search)
- Licenses are "grandfathered" in
- Goodwill
- Technology, clients, and vendors are instantly acquired
- Negotiations usually take place on top level, target handles licensing and compliance
- Instant branding
- Reduction of competition
- Increased knowledge base

CONS:

- Hidden surprises?

- Which employees are politically connected, and with whom?

- "Favors" and concessions are assumed

- Bad will

- Technology often outmoded, vendors usually chosen for reasons besides merit

- In many nations, employment continuance becomes conditional for the deal

- Branding often not part of HQ's ideals

- Often expensive, and time consuming to complete an acquisition

- Blending of corporate cultures

- Necessity to train local management, and HQ's management

- Potential tax and legal problems

THINGS TO CONSIDER:

- Half the merged entities never achieve their projected financial and market goals.

- A merger may mean short-term cash, but not necessarily future stability

- Existing business problems, synergy problems, staff problems

- Buying an overvalued company

- How should you finance the acquisition – cash or stock?

2. GREENFIELD INVESTMENT:

A project that starts with bare ground and builds up from there. Coca Cola, McDonalds, and Starbucks are great examples of American companies that have invested in Greenfield projects around the world.

PROS:

- Economies of scale and scope in production, marketing, finance, research and development, transportation, and purchasing

- Greater control in all aspects

- Best long term strategy

- Commitment to market

- Vendor financing often available

- Work with authorities from the beginning

- Control over your brand

- Control over staff

- Press opportunities

CONS:

- Higher expense,

- Competition in these markets can be difficult to over-come,

- Entry into these markets can take years to happen

- Barriers to entry can be costly

- Governmental regulations may put these multinational enterprises at a disadvantage in the short term

3. LICENSING:

A contractual arrangement whereby a company transfers via a license, the right to distribute or manufacture a product or service to a foreign country or to use any type of expertise which may include some or all of the following: patents, trademarks, company name, technology/technological know-how, design, and/or business methods. The licensee pays a fee and/or percentage of sales in exchange for the rights.

ADVANTAGEOUS WHEN:

Import and investment barriers exist, when legal protection is possible in the target environment, when there is otherwise, a low sales potential in target country or a large cultural distance is present.

PROS:

- Quick and easy entry into foreign markets: allows a company to 'jump' border and tariff barriers.

- Lower capital requirements

- Potential for a large ROI; returns are realized fairly quickly

- Risks are very low with this mode of market entry. You can enter with an established product; avoid most "uncontrollable" risks and have fewer financial and legal risks

CONS:

- Control by the licensee is low

- The licensee may become a competitor

- Intellectual property may be lost

- License period is usually limited

- Poor management of quality, for example, can damage brand reputation in other license territories

A. TECHNOLOGY LICENSING:

When a licensor's patents, trademarks, service marks, copyrights, trade secrets, or other intellectual property may be sold or made available to a licensee for compensation that is negotiated in advance between the parties.

PROS:

- This mode can provide 'reverse flow' of technology in which the original licensor shares in technical improvements developed by the licensee

- Licensee is able to use the intangible property and receive technical assistance

CONS:

- This can yield loss of control over technology

- Potential loss of intellectual property

- Control over the technology is weakened because it has been transferred to an unaffiliated firm

B. FRANCHISING:

This can be a very efficient model for distributing goods and services. In this type of licensing agreement, control over the operations is granted to the franchisee in exchange for some type of payment and for the promise to abide by the terms of the contract.

PROS:

- Market entry with less financial, legal, and political risks; working with proven product

- Economies of scale by ordering with owner and other franchisees

- Partners can come to the new market and see the business up close, first hand

CONS:

- The licensor has little direct control

- Licensee has lower profits than if owned business or exported own goods

4. FOREIGN DIRECT INVESTMENT:

FDI is direct ownership of facilities in the target country. It may be made through the acquisition of an existing entity or the establishment of a new enterprise. There is a high degree of commitment and high level of resources. Japanese automobile manufacturers are well known for their use of wholly owned subsidiaries in the USA.

ADVANTAGEOUS WHEN:

There are import barriers; there is a small cultural distance; assets cannot be fairly priced; there are high sales potential; low political risk exists.

PROS:

- Provides high degree of control in the operations

- The ability to better know the consumers and competitive environment (a direct presence)

- Provides jobs in target country. Governments will help you!

- Provides the scale economies and efficiencies of production when across several markets

- Benefit of the comparative advantage of different economies such as the supply of labor or raw materials

- Has value of technology ownership (minimizes technology spill-overs)

- Your firm is considered to be an "insider"

CONS:

- Higher risks; this entry strategy has the highest capital and management costs

- Greater difficulty in managing local resources

- The largest array of uncontrollable factors affects the foreign direct investor including currency and exchange risks, performance requirement risks, discriminatory tax, and licensing requirements, to name a few

5. JOINT VENTURES:

A cooperative between two or more organizations that share a common interest in a business enterprise or undertaking; is a popular mode for quick entry.

A. EXAMPLE OF INTERNATIONAL COMPANY AND LOCAL OWNERS:

General Mills teamed up with Nestlé to form Cereal Partners Worldwide in an effort to compete against Kellogg in the European cereal market.

General Mills brought strong cereal brand names, technology and expertise to the table while Nestlé brought European manufacturing facilities and a strong distribution system.

Each separate company had something different to offer and the resulting combination allowed the joint venture to flourish.

As shown in the example, the local company, Nestlé, had existing business infrastructure in the proposed market and, therefore, had knowledge of the customs and tastes of the people. This advantage allowed General Mills to enter the market more quickly than if it had chosen to build a manufacturing facility from scratch. Some other advantages of such a joint venture include gained political contacts, lower tax rates on profits, fewer inspections and less government interference in daily operations, greater assurance of continuous electricity supplies, more local infrastructure such as roads and utilities and easier access to government controlled raw materials and supplies.

Attached is a preliminary PDF design of the 3-ring binder concept. There are some improvements to be made and a few elements still to be "stylized". Our goal before starting production would be to have a standard style guide for all elements, which shouldn't take too much to complete. One example of a change is we have a new way we want to treat the breakers.

Joint ventures, like any other mode of entry, come with some associated drawbacks. Loss of effective management control can be a major disadvantage of the joint venture with a local owner. It is common for developing nations to require that the local owner hold majority ownership of a joint venture. In this instance, it is obvious that the local owner will have a greater say in business decisions and their lack of expertise could result in reduced profits, increased operating costs, inferior product quality, exposure to product liability or even environmental litigation and fines. Shared profits are another huge disadvantage of the joint venture. Neither General Mills nor Nestlé gets to keep all of the profits of Cereal Partners Worldwide. Finally, the loss of intellectual property is a drawback that should be considered before entering a joint venture with a local owner. As a result of forming Cereal Partners Worldwide, Nestlé now knows much more about producing the General Mills line than they did before the agreement. The pros and cons must be weighed before any joint venture should be established.

B. EXAMPLE OF TWO INTERNATIONAL COMPANIES JOINING FOR BUSINESS IN A THIRD MARKET:

Ford and Volkswagen teamed up in 1987 to form Autolatina in an effort to sell cars in South America. Autolatina produced vehicles that were based on Ford and Volkswagen designs but marketed through each respective manufacturer's distribution channels. The advantages of such an agreement include the increased resources and expertise gained by each participant as well as the shared risk between the companies.

The obvious drawback of this type of joint venture is that neither company may have an existing foothold in the third market. In this regard, the process may be similar to starting a business from the ground up, which is extremely costly and time consuming. The remaining disadvantages are similar to other types of joint ventures in that both companies will lose some management control, some profits, and some intellectual property during the agreement.

C. EXAMPLE OF AN INTERNATIONAL COMPANY AND A GOVERNMENT ENTITY:

This is a lesser-used mode of joint venture. This type of agreement has been used extensively by the various states of the former Soviet Union. Tengizchevroil is a joint venture between Chevron and Kazakhstan to produce, refine, and transport oil for both domestic use and sale abroad. The oil is located in Kazakhstan and Chevron has the expertise and equipment to run the entire operation.

The advantages for Chevron include a virtually unhindered access to the market, ease of licensing and tax benefits. The advantages for Kazakhstan are just as obvious. The former Soviet republic gets expert production of its oil, newly created jobs, and profits.

The disadvantages to Chevron include the hardships in dealing with the unstable political, economical, and legal framework; the difficulty in accessing the pipeline for transport, and the extremely high and uncertain export taxes on oil leaving Kazakhstan. Chevron might also have to deal with a government that is not concerned with profit. In other words, Kazakhstan may not care about keeping production high so long as oil is being produced.

D. EXAMPLE OF TWO OR MORE INTERNATIONAL COMPANIES FOR A LIMITED DURATION PROJECT:

This is a very popular mode of entry. This mode can be demonstrated best by considering a construction project in

Turkey. Bechtel Group established a joint venture with Enka Insaat va Sanayi to construct the 229-kilometer Ankara-Gerede Highway in Turkey. The agreement outlined the duties of each respective company in regard to financing, project management, procurement, hiring, design, subcontracting and administration.

The advantages of this type of joint venture again include shared risk and expertise and increased resources. An excellent by-product of this agreement is the upgraded skill level of the countrymen as a result of the work. The Ankara-Gerede Highway project employed nearly 6,000 Turkish workers, some of which arrived not knowing how to drive a car and left as expert operators of multimillion-dollar equipment.

The major drawbacks are similar to other joint ventures along the lines of shared profits, loss of complete control, and potential loss of intellectual property.

6. EXPORTING

A. DIRECT:

Selling a product or service directly to a foreign firm by the home-country firm. Costs and prices may be lowest if production occurs in only a few locations around the world and the efficiently produced goods are exported to most markets. Pharmaceutical and clothing companies use this mode frequently for globalizing.

- Sales Representatives/Paid by seller: foreign-based representatives who work on a salary/retainer plus incentive basis to locate buyers for a company's products.

- Distributors/Agents: purchase merchandise directly from the home-country firm to re-sell at a profit.

- Direct Sales to End-User: A manufacturer of medical equipment, for example, may be able to sell directly to hospitals. Other major end-users include foreign governments, schools, businesses and individual consumers.

ADVANTAGEOUS WHEN:

There is limited sales potential in target country; little product adaptation is required; distribution channels are close to plants; there are high target-country production costs; there are liberal import policies; high political risk exists.

PROS:

- No investment in foreign production facilities is required

- Maintain more control, minimized risk and investment, speedy entry

- Maximize economies of scale; to prevent competitors from gaining 'first-mover' advantages in new markets

- Sell excess production capacity

- Gain information about foreign competition

- Stabilize seasonal market fluctuations

- Reduces dependence on existing markets

CONS:

- This can be more expensive due to tariffs, marketing expenses, transport costs

- It may be difficult to coordinate the cooperation of exporter, importer, transport provider, and government

- Limited access to local information; company viewed as "outsider"

- Need to develop customer base and logistics of moving the goods overseas

- May be difficult to overcome trade barriers

- May lose control over product's pricing and marketing

- Task of finding customers

B. INDIRECT:

Selling goods and services through various types of intermediaries.

- Foreign agents are hired by companies for representation in overseas markets as the agent has knowledge of business practices, language, laws, and culture. There are different types of agents who perform a number of functions. The one you choose to hire is based upon how much you want the agent to do for you and how much you are willing to pay.

- Exporters use commissioned agents most often. It is the simplest way of doing things: The agent is paid a percentage of a sale only when the sale is made. This provides an incentive for the agent to work on your behalf.

- Retainer agents are paid a fixed amount to do certain work for a company over a specified period of time. The disadvantage is that it is difficult to monitor how hard they are working and they get paid whether they do anything or not.

- Retainer/Commissioned agents are placed on a retainer but also receive a percentage from each sale. The retainer provides them with funds to help run their business while the commission gives them additional incentive to work harder on your behalf.

PROS: AGENTS CAN:

- Help identify customers for your products and market your goods to them

- Uncover other opportunities/ markets for your product

- Translate and act as interpreter in business dealings in the foreign country

- Validate translation of your publicity materials

- Assist with local travel and/or living arrangements

- Provide guidance with local government regulations.

CONS:

- Agents often work for other businesses…and truly work for the BUYER, not the seller

- Agents prioritize their clients based on product, incentives and/or base pay

- There are no guarantees the agents will make inroads in terms of market share with your product

2. EXPORT MANAGEMENT COMPANY (EMC):

Functions as an "off-site" export sales department, representing your product along with various other non-competitive manufacturers. The EMC searches for business for your company and usually provides the following services: market research and development of marketing strategy; locating new, and utilizing existing foreign distributors or sales representatives to put your product into the foreign market. Functions as an overseas distribution channel or wholesaler. Takes ownership of the goods and operates on a commission basis.

PROS:

- Faster entry into the overseas market in terms of first recorded sales

- Better focus on exporting because most firms give priority to their domestic problems

- Lower out-of-pocket expenses

- An opportunity to study the methods and potential of exporting; expertise in dealing with the special details involved in exporting, as well as its strategies

CONS:

- No control of the export strategies and quality control of after-sales service

- Can create competition from the EMC's/ETC's other products (might be more profitable and easier to sell)

- Reluctance of some foreign buyers to deal with a third-party intermediary

- Added costs and higher selling prices because of gross profit margin requirements of the EMC/ETC, unless the economies of scale can be used to offset this factor

3. PIGGYBACK EXPORTING:

When a company, which already has an export distribution system in place, is allowed to sell another company's product in addition to its own. A good advantage is that the requisite logistics associated with selling abroad are borne by the exporting company.

PROS:

- International experience not required

- Fast entry to the international market

- Lower increased financial commitment; generally lower risk

CONS:

- Low control by the exporting business

- Possible choice of wrong market, wrong distributor

- Inadequate market feedback

- Potentially lower sales

- Higher risk in general

- Brand erosion

7. E-COMMERCE:

Using inter-networked computers to create and transform business relationships. Applications provide business solutions that improve the quality of goods and services, increase the speed of service delivery, and reduce the cost of business operations. A new methodology of doing business in three focal areas:

- Business-to-business

- Business-to-consumer

- Intra-business

It is most commonly associated with buying and selling information, products, and services via the Internet, but it is also used to transfer and share information within organizations through intranets to improve decision-making and eliminate duplication of effort. The new paradigm of

E-Commerce is built not just on transactions but also on building, sustaining, and improving relationships, both existing and potential. Companies like Dell Computer, Toys-R-Us, Ebay and Yahoo have found E-Commerce a viable business model. With an estimated $900 billion expected in E-Commerce in 2010, this type of business relationship is here to stay.

PROS:

- Quick, easy way to increase market share; if correct marketing methodologies are employed

- Easy way to gain a "presence" in international markets

- After capital costs paid off, productivity, and therefore, profits increase

- Enables greater economies of scale

CONS:

- Hardware and software are essential, and these are big expenses

- Distribution must be very efficient

- Website needs constant updates, which leads to extra labor, training, and retraining costs

- True costs of E-business difficult to calculate

- Much less trust than "click and brick" entities

8. WHOLLY OWNED SUBSIDIARY (WOS):

Entails a direct investment in the target country. Wholly owned operations are subsidiaries in another nation in which the parent company has full ownership and sole responsibility for the management of the operation. Eastman Kodak has WOSs in many countries.

ADVANTAGEOUS WHEN:

Risks of investing in a particular foreign market are low, maximum operational control is desired; when host governments have open trade and investment policies.

PROS:

- Highest level of control
- Lowest technology risk
- High performance
- Best long-term strategy, with the possible exception of Greenfield entry

CONS:

- High investment risk
- High resource commitment
- Generally higher tax rates on profits
- More regulated; government interference in daily operations
- Lots of planning required

- Slow entry

- May have more difficulty accessing local government-controlled raw materials and supplies

- Some countries feel exploited with this type of method

9. CONTRACT MANUFACTURING:

A firm contracts with a local manufacturer to produce its products to the firm's specifications. An example of this is when Gates Rubber licensed one of its belt technologies to General Tire's Chilean plant. General Tire produced part of its output with Gates' label. Take the case of Peace Frogs T-shirts who exports T-shirts directly to many countries. However, in Spain per capita income is lower, competition from domestic producers is stronger and tariffs are high. Peace Frogs they license a Barcelona-based company the rights to manufacture their product.

ADVANTAGEOUS WHEN:

Risks of investing in a foreign country are high, when there are stringent import barriers, when high political risks exist, lack of raw materials at home.

PROS:

- Frequently importation of like products is halted but the firm contracting manufacturing would earn a royalty on the now locally produced product, would have belts made to their specifications without the expense of investing in production facilities, and competition of other importers would be eliminated

- Generates employment and foreign exchange for the host country

- Usually easy access to entry as host country knows laws, politics, customs, and can begin to build a relationship within the host country

CONS:

- Could lose control of quality; possible low quality workers

- No control of pricing or marketing

- No equity in the subcontractor

- Your competition may be a customer!

10. MANAGEMENT CONTRACT:

When one firm provides management in all or specific areas for another firm, in exchange for a fee. Hilton Hotels, for example, provides management services for non-owned overseas hotels that use the Hilton name. In return, Hilton probably earns a fee that is a percentage of sales and, more importantly, gains brand recognition. Similarly, Delta Airlines also provides management services to foreign airlines in exchange for a fee.

PROS:

- Entry to the market is rather simple

- Using business experience to help similar companies in other countries is easy to set up, operate, and collect on

- It also allows the experienced company an opportunity to research the market for other modes of entry

CONS:

- Lack of profit; a percentage of sales are not typically the largest margin possible when operating a business

- The foreign company will gain much insight into the business procedures of the expert company

- Detrimental to the expert company in the long run if the foreign firm ever becomes a competitor

A. TURN-KEY PROJECT:

This can also be a form of contract management. This is when aspects of a business are contracted and then run for a specified amount of time until the purchaser takes over. Aspects of the project can be coordinated from inception through completion. These processes can include technology, design, construction, or providing expertise in a particular area.

11. STRATEGIC ALLIANCES:

An often-overlooked mode of entry is the strategic alliance. This is typically a business relationship where similar companies combine efforts to get a better price on materials, perform research and development, collaborate on marketing or distribution, or even seek new business. A good example of a strategic alliance took place in 1997 between Intel, Motorola, and Advanced Micro Devices. The three separate corporations formed a not-for-profit company called Extreme Ultraviolet in order to collaborate on research and development.

Strategic alliances aim to achieve advantages of scale, scope and speed, increase market penetration, increase competitiveness, enhance product development, develop new business opportunities and markets, increase exports and reduce costs.

The main drawback of any strategic alliance is the potential for the alliance to be taken over by one of the partners. Since the partners are most often competitors, there is always a chance that the alliance will break up in the end.

Entering or expanding in a foreign market can obviously be accomplished through a wide variety of different options. A mode of entry should be selected only after analyzing each alternative and comparing it to others.

The three basic differentiating characteristics between the modes of entry are:

- The quantity of resource commitment required

- The amount of control

- The level of risk

In general, exporting requires the least amount of resources and allows for the lowest level of control. Wholly owned subsidiaries, on the other hand, require the most resources but allow for the most control. As far as technology risk is concerned, exporting is the least risky while licensing is generally the most risky. It is apparent that not every mode of entry will work for every situation. A company looking to enter a foreign market should look at the experiences of other companies in similar markets to try and gain some insight as to the best alternative. During the process and additionally, after the choice of entry has been made, the company should definitely enlist the help of a professional such as an international marketer to insure the best possible strategy is carried out. The most control is usually what is sought, however, control can be expensive.

THE PROCESS:

Mode of entry (MOE) should be carefully determined. The determinants are:

THE HOST FIRM'S

- Current business model
- Access to capital
- Attitude towards risk
- Pay back rate and period

THE MARKET'S

- Accepted means of doing business
- Hole or niche in the market

- Competitive modes of entry and their success/failure rates

- Differentiation of product and service

- The issues should be discussed strategically. It is best to set aside some days with visiting expertise to uncover means for market entry, and begin to understand the risk factors and budgeting process.

COSTS:

- Budget should be created to complete the research stage of the project

- Once research has backed the MOE, legal, tax, and regulatory advice may be necessary

- Depending on MOE, direct sales research, partner approach, acquisition evaluations, or distribution channel research should be committed. If Greenfield site, budgeting team needs to be established

- Budget should be augmented based on information gained

- Project team (inside and outside) should be chosen; work divided

- Site analysis in new market to begin

- Market distribution courted

- Final decision (and budget created) on MOE undertaken

- Full costs understood

- Market entry team selected
- Market entry team trained

DISCLAIMER

These articles were published between 2005 and 2011 and contain "how to" strategies for companies engaged in global business. Obviously, many of the facts and figures have changed but the concepts are as valid today as they were several years ago.

My Archive of "How To" Articles from the Denver Business Journal

10 MYTHS ABOUT ENTERING INTERNATIONAL MARKETS

Here are 10 misconceptions by companies about entering overseas markets.

IF WE MAKE A BETTER MOUSETRAP, THEY WILL BUY IT.

The question here is, do you think that factor alone is the necessary and sufficient condition to sell overseas? If it was always about quality, then why doesn't everyone always buy the best product?

Many overseas buyers will purchase an inferior product from someone who has a closer relationship with them, knows their business and culture, and understands them personally.

The sales cycle can take a great deal of time, because the customer intimacy takes time to develop. Contrast this to the United States, where we often change vendors without a second thought.

ENGLISH IS THE UNIVERSAL LANGUAGE, SO WE CAN SIMPLY SELL IN ENGLISH.

This speaks to several issues: Does everyone in the client organization speak, read and write English? Remember, decisions often are made on a consensus basis, and your marketing materials may travel quite a bit within the clients' firms and sit on many desks.

And even if everyone in the company is comfortable with English, why not take the extra step and make it easy for them to buy (instead of easy for you to sell)? Translating materials is one of the simplest and most effective ways to show investment into a market, and will differentiate you from your competitors, who make no effort at all. Speaking the local language (at least enough to apologize for not speaking it) will help greatly.

OUR LABOR COST IS TOO HIGH TO MARKET OUR PRODUCT OVERSEAS.

This myth can be refuted with one statistic: Fifty-five percent of Japan's trade surplus with the United States comes from industries where their labor cost is higher than ours. If labor cost was the deciding factor, then how on earth could Germany possibly sell anything abroad? Why aren't we simply buying everything (from automobiles to wine to satellites) from Zimbabwe, where the labor cost is among the lowest?

OUR PRICE IS TOO HIGH FOR OVERSEAS MARKETS.

Are you intending to compete only on price? Many commodities (oil, wheat, cement, corn) are price-sensitive, but the vast majority of international successes aren't. Ipod is successful around the globe (and certainly not the low-cost option), as are Mercedes, BMW, Coca Cola and Tanqueray. In many cultures (e.g. Japan, Korea), service would be the differentiator.

74

OUR SKILLED MARKETERS CAN TAKE ON OVERSEAS MAR-KETS.

If we define marketing as awareness, understanding and belief, we need to ask:

Do my marketing people know how to make overseas markets aware of the product? Do they know how to explain the products, attributes and benefits in terms that make sense to the locals?

Can they convince overseas buyers of the merits of working with your company? Do they understand how markets are organized and how buying decisions are made?

OUR IN-HOUSE FOREIGN NATIONALS CAN SELL TO OVER-SEAS MARKETS.

In one example, a U.S.-based CEO told me his Chinese wife could negotiate with the Chinese government for market entry. My questions were: Is she a skilled negotiator? Does she understand the sales process? Does she have the motivation and energy to break into this difficult market?

Does she have the correct contacts and support needed to gain entry? Does she understand how to navigate the Chinese system? Language and cultural skills alone don't suffice.

OUR LOCAL PARTNERS WILL HANDLE ALL OF THE MAR-KETING.

This idea of relinquishing market control while enjoying great success is rare. Most of the time, overseas partners will look toward the parent to help stimulate demand, deal with problems as they occur, get to know the distribution channels, offer subject matter expertise indeed invested in the market.

THE CUSTOMER EXPRESSED ALL OF THE BUYING SIGNS, AND EVEN SAID "YES" TO OUR PROPOSAL.

Many firms overseas conduct their market research by posing as buyers. They conduct competitive intelligence the same way. Your banker will tell you that the sale is complete only when the money has been deposited into the bank.

"Yes" when uttered in business meetings may simply mean "I understand you," not acceptance of your proposal.

WE DON'T NEED TO INVEST A LOT; OUR WEB SITE GIVES US A PRESENCE.

Actually, your Web site gives you a brochure, but no real place where businesses and consumers can get support, touch and feel your product, get to know your company and its staff, deal with returns, make product modifications and enable co-marketing agreements.

It's necessary to have a localized Web site for market presence, but it needs to accompany many other things to make your efforts a success.

IF IT WORKED HERE (IN THE UNITED STATES), IT WILL WORK THERE.

This speaks to local ethnocentrism. Success at home also can be a hindrance to overseas success. Arrogance and impatience are often by products of domestic success. Market conditions, buying conditions, business practices, negotiation tactics and product specifications all differ by market.

The firms that realize this quickly always will have the advantage.

BEWARE OF THE HUMAN RESOURCES LAWS OVERSEAS

Have you ever wondered why you see people in the pubs in Europe all day? When we walk around American cities, at 2:30 p.m. people are working and the restaurants are empty.

Yet, in Paris, Amsterdam, London or Rome, we see locals having coffee or drinks, socializing during normal working hours. What are the reasons for this?

First of all, the locals may not work the kinds of hours we Americans do. It's quite possible that the people you see sipping Cinzano are off the clock. Germans average a 35-hour work week, so you could be catching the "Hoffbrau Haus crowd" after a shift at work.

HOWEVER, THERE ARE ALTERNATE EXPLANATIONS.

- One could be that the people working are actually supposed to be at work, at their desks. In several countries, employers can't ask about the whereabouts of their staff on a continuous basis. They must show cause of their concerns to appropriate "work councils."

- Another reason could be that the people are, in fact, working. Meetings in coffee shops are not uncommon in the United States. Cafés in Europe have a business culture as well.

- But another rationale for the 3 p.m. pub crowd could be that the people you see not working have been terminated by their employers – yet continue to receive paychecks. Those paychecks can be up to 80 percent of the salary the employee would receive if they were working.

The human resources atmosphere in many countries obligates employers to commit to an employee with a "permanent contract."

This seems strange to Americans. U.S. companies do pay into unemployment benefits, and discharged employees often receive unemployment checks for a set period.

In Europe, those unemployment laws are much more stringent and employee-friendly. And employers may be paying a much larger share (50 percent isn't uncommon) into the unemployment fund. Naturally, rules are country-specific, but remember that socialized (therefore subsidized) health care and free university tuition are common benefits available to everyone in most Western European countries.

The money has to come from somewhere: high personal income taxes and enormous corporate taxes and fees.

As an example: In Austria, when one opens a bank account with 1,000 Euros, it magically becomes about 920 Euros after the bank takes all of its fees. Once a bank deposit is made, the bank will be subject to various government fees.

French students are protesting the peeling back of worker benefits. If France wishes to compete on a world scale in any industry that's dependent on high labor content, then

CEOs need to be able to hire and fire at will. When large-client orders come in, a firm needs to be able to bring on more people. When business slows down, companies can't survive unless they can reduce their variable costs.

But in France, labor always was seen as a fixed cost.

With the French government as a partner in most French industries, firms exist not only to provide value to customers, but also to provide jobs.

The HR issues extend way beyond employment. They can include what you can (and can't) ask of an employee. Laws may encompass work hours, counter heights, safety equipment, desk space, smoking permission, travel restriction and bathroom facilities.

For example: German mothers receive one full year of maternity leave from their employers. And no one can be terminated for being pregnant.

In the United States, we believe we're one of the more progressive, humane countries. We can't ask personal questions (sex, religion) on job applications.

YET EUROPEANS OFTEN CALL AMERICAN EMPLOYEES THREE-TIME LOSERS:

- First, we often mortgage our homes (in our 50s) to pay for children's college educations, compared to free education for Europeans.

- Second, employers can terminate us at that age, while many Europeans enjoy either lifetime employment or lifetime income regardless of employment.

- Third, since our health care is often tied to American employers, losing our jobs means losing our coverage. Our European counterparts receive socialized medicine provided by their governments, regardless of employer. The European HR squeeze therefore does have its purpose.

HOW CAN U.S. FIRMS ENTERING FOREIGN MARKETS ESCAPE SOME OF THE HR BIND?

- Use consultants, not employees. The Netherlands (which numbers about 16 million people) employs more management consultants than the United States, precisely because of HR laws.

- Seek small entrepreneurial firms instead of employees, as you may not be able to terminate employees easily (depending on the country).

- Find a partner, a firm that complements your business. Let the partner deal with the local laws.

- Employ the foreigner you wish in the United States, and send them back overseas to work. Depending on the country, this person may have to reside in the United States for a part of each month or year.

- Find people who understand these issues during your due diligence.

DON'T LET INTERMEDIARY
IMPEDE YOUR IMPORTING SUCCESS

What does a global procurement officer from a large technology firm in Boulder and a hobbyist selling dresses from Argentina have in common?

They're both importers, taking goods from a foreign country and bringing them into the United States. Importers range in size, scope and specialty. But they all share the same potential pitfalls and roadblocks.

There are two main ways to import: directly and though intermediaries. The intermediary may be called a trading company, importer, buyer's representative, agent or a host of other titles.

THERE ARE SEVERAL ADVANTAGES TO USING AN INTERMEDIARY:

- They tend to know what they're doing.

- They understand the exporting country's language, culture and business practices.

- Intermediaries know how deals are done and can avoid complications.

- Intermediaries may do much business with factories you're interested in. Hence, they may have larger buying power and receive better service.

- They often offer one-stop shopping (freight, customs, arranging payment, perhaps even quality control).

- They often have relationships with factories, so they can find suppliers with greater ease.

- They should save you time.

HOWEVER, THERE ARE MANY DISADVANTAGES TO USING AN INTERMEDIARY:

- They charge for this service. Often a buyer has no idea how much they're paying this person. Trading companies may say they're being paid by the seller (and that may be who writes the check), but in reality the buyer is putting all the cash into the deal.

- The best intermediaries will try to keep some mud in the transaction, never revealing the true costs and terms.

- Often, trading companies work with friends of theirs or other preferred suppliers who may reward them better than other suppliers. This means the buyer may not be getting the best deal.

- Intermediaries try to keep the buyer and seller apart. Think of buying a house through brokers. They wish to handle all the transactions and never allow the buyer and seller to meet. This means the buyer and seller never develop a relationship.

On a one-time deal like purchasing a house, this may be acceptable. But if you're running a company that's dependent on constant flows of imported product, it's always best to build a strong relationship with your supplier.

- Other deals can suffer. When using an intermediary, you get to see only one side of the supplier's business. Maybe the supplier can benefit from doing other deals with you (consulting agreements, inventory control processes, importing your products into their market and co-branding relationships all come to mind).

The intermediary, however, will sell from his bag and not necessarily look at other revenue streams that can emerge.

- Organizational learning suffers. The buyer never gets the savvy to effectively do other deals in other places because they're always relying on the intermediary.

Enno Fritz, president of Euro Espresso Imports in Lakewood, which imports high-end coffee-roasting and coffee-making equipment from Europe, has been a direct importer for many years.

He cautions it's essential for the overseas factory to understand the U.S. marketing plan if they're to work together. "They need to understand the plan, and understand your business," Fritz says.

Almost every factory he's dealt with in Europe has had failures in the U.S. market. "This is usually because (e.g.) Italian manufacturers will prefer to deal with an Italian national in the U.S. That person may not be a good importer and marketer, but gets the factory's trust because of nationality."

Fritz therefore stresses that good importers need to overcome this nationalistic prejudice and make sure they go to the factories, get to know the people and explain the market strategy.

Another common problem is that since foreign factories don't understand the U.S. market, they rely on the importer to educate them. However, an importer may feel that the less the factory knows about the U.S. market, the more power he has.

Fritz disagrees with this approach. He said there should be a partnership with the factory in the market. The importer can discuss things such as where the factory can invest money, which product modifications will do well locally and which trade shows should be attended.

FRITZ ALSO MAKES FOUR MAJOR CAUTIONS TO POTENTIAL IMPORTERS:

- Be careful of new products. Make sure they're released at the appropriate time and the market has accepted any modifications.

- Order the right amount of product. Order enough to make the sales you need, but never so much product that the market changes or your capital gets consumed in unneeded inventory.

- Try not to own the product for too long. If the factory owns the product while it sits in your warehouse, it will be more inclined to repair, modify or replace product when needed. When importers own product, it becomes the importer's problem.

- Last, try not to be in a situation in which you're fighting both the factory and the market forces.

HOW NOT TO BE AN UGLY
AMERICAN WHEN YOU TRAVEL OVERSEAS

Let's face it; Americans have a terrible reputation abroad.

We have controversial foreign policies. Time after time we have elected monolingual presidents (our Congress is mostly monolingual as well). We live with huge domestic problems such as homelessness, lack of health insurance, violent street crime and high school graduates who can't read.

Europeans laugh at the fact that Americans can earn an M.B.A. degree in international business without owning a passport. That doesn't happen in Europe – most European M.B.A. degree-holders are multilingual and much-traveled.

The world's business press reports on American bankruptcies where the company directors seem to destroy shareholders, employees and creditors alike – and yet seemingly pay no penalty.

In overseas marketing, we fail an astonishing 82 percent of the time.

Our ethnocentrism is apparent. The United States is the only nation that refers to a national sporting championship as "The World Series." Our executives travel abroad without knowing anything at all about the host county's politics, history or language.

We often refer to the Czech Republic as being in Eastern Europe (it's really central Europe), and confuse terms such as socialism and communism.

Our massive marketing machine, coveted media properties, and influence in the English language abroad can convince us the world wants to be American, buy American and act American.

A great example of this is the presence of Marlboro cigarettes around the world. This product is so successful that it doesn't seem to matter that no one can pronounce it. It would be healthy to regard this as an interesting exception, not the rule.

Marlboro also enjoys a rather substantial marketing budget (bigger than most country's GDPs).

Foreign countries regard many of our visible exports – unhealthy foods, tobacco, firearms, TV and video violence – as vices. Hence, many of our marketing successes have strong push back abroad, and many are asking us to stop exporting some of our concepts.

GIVEN THAT AMERICANS ARE STARTING OUT AT A DISADVANTAGE, HOW CAN WE AVOID BEING AN UGLY AMERICAN?

- Read about where you're going to transact business. Learn some of the history, business practices and characters. Don't set foot in a country without knowing who its leaders are.

- Learn enough of the local language to at least apologize for not speaking it.

- Don't let the presence of Hooters in Shanghai or Mountain Dew in Kuala Lumpur let you believe these countries have abandoned their values and mind sets.

- When speaking, avoid sporting and military analogies. "Who is quarterbacking this?" "get a ballpark figure" and "we need a home run on this" are often unintelligible to overseas business people.

And remember, the sport that we call "soccer," most everyone else calls "football." "Let's run it up the flagpole and see who salutes it" can offend.

- Avoid politics whenever possible (it's not always possible). Politics and business are linked in most countries, so it becomes necessary to play ambassador when negotiating abroad.

When U.S. actions are brought up, a good way out is to explain that you were never consulted. Think of other useful phrases and techniques to avoid committing to ideologies.

- If you're going to do business with them, you must understand them. You also must commit to them.

- Remember, your overseas counterparts probably know more about your culture than you know about theirs. Rectify this by reading, asking questions of experts before you travel and engaging your counterparts in intellectual discussions while you're there.

- Never do the classic American "10 countries in eight days business trip." It's better to spend the entire 10 days in one country and really make an attempt to get to know your counterparts.

If they're distributing your products, meet their customers. If they're manufacturing your products, understand how they operate. If they're promoting your ideas, figure out how you can help them, and be in town long enough to assist them.

If you have only 10 days to travel to see everyone, then you're not the best person to do business for your firm abroad. Dedicated, executive time will differentiate you.

- Translate your materials into the local language (s). Your card, brochures, collateral materials, etc. should be easily understood by the locals.

- Don't leave without telling your local counterparts when you're coming back. This shows commitment on your part. However, it also allows your local hosts to make plans for your next trip, whether it's blocking time for you, setting up meetings or preparing demonstrations.

- When discussing religion (again, often linked with business), try to do so with an open mind.

- Show curiosity. If you're not genuinely curious about other countries' cultures, politics and religious beliefs, then you probably don't belong there in the first place.

HERE'S WHY PARTNERSHIPS CAN LEAD TO BIG PROBLEMS

When entering foreign markets, many firms use the partner approach. But surprisingly, so few firms pick the correct ones.

The most common American model is to find a competitor in a foreign market, approach it and try to develop a partnership. The venture can take many forms, from a traditional merger to an arm's-length agreement to work together. Referring to a "partner" is not a sufficient definition of the relationship.

PARTNERSHIPS BREED PROBLEMS, AND WE NEED TO KNOW WHY.

In one case, an American oil firm partnered with a firm based in Alberta, Canada. The purpose was to corroborate on deals in new markets. Canadian firms were obvious choices for the Americans; no language barrier, geographically desirable, transparent legal systems and some common business values.

The Canadian firm had capital and access to more funding. Additionally, the Canadians had comparable technology and a greater international outlook.

Canadians already think more globally than Americans. The country has two official languages – cereal boxes are labeled in English and in French. Most Canadians live within 50 miles of the U.S. border. American news is prominent on Canadian television and radio, and in newspapers. One of every six Canadians is an immigrant. More than 50 percent of Canadians have traveled abroad (compared with less than 10 percent for the United States).

When the Canadians landed a deal in Central Europe, the Americans (who weren't germane to the negotiations) called the Canadians and asked, "Are we in? What is our role in this new deal?"

This question surprised and confused the Canadians. The U.S. firm committed no resources, help, money or contacts to this venture, yet were hoping to reap the rewards. The Americans were equally daunted, as they felt the Canadians would include their firm in most overseas activities.

The true logistics obviously weren't solidified. But the main reason for failure was that the collaboration wasn't grounded in each firm's needs. Each company offered duplicative strengths. With each party bringing the same skills to the table, the only logical reason for the parties to connect seemed to be to form a gentleman's alliance.

As we examine what went wrong, we need to ask: What makes a partnership successful in the first place? One of the biggest success factors is a common outlook on how the partnership will function. Additionally, a common understanding of the tasks at hand, complementary skills, and co-mingling of talent, technology and contacts are good places to start.

For instance, if the Canadians offered superior technology, yet the Americans had access to more capital, then that would be a good basis for joining. In this example, the Canadians didn't need the Americans to help service Canadian firms, and the reverse held true for the Americans. Their only hope was to cooperate on international deals. Yet the Canadians went about this business activity on their own.

If the Canadians were better at international business development, then why did they need the Americans anyway?

Perhaps the indirectness of the Canadian culture versus the U.S. cards-on-the-table approach increased ambiguity. Perhaps the Canadian reticence versus the American aggressiveness made the Canadians think the U.S. company would present opportunities first.

SO, HOW IS A GOOD PARTNER CHOSEN?

First, the partners have to research each other. They need to know each other's strength and weakness, how easy will cooperation be, and each other's agendas (defined by the question: What does success look like?).

Common goals and agreed-upon action plans for attaining them should be decided, negotiated, assigned and monitored. In international business, remember that most countries are hierarchical, thus, a firm would want to select another that is hierarchically well placed.

For example, professors are located near the top of Chinese society (above doctors, lawyers, factory bosses and bankers). Politicians are regarded highly in India, engineers in The Netherlands and entertainers in the United States.

By working with those at the top of their society, foreigners piggyback in on several advantages: government cooperation, existing clients, the grandfathering of licenses and

Western- trained talent. The trick is to know beforehand what hierarchies exist in which countries. Then learn how to get to those desirable entities before your competitors do.

To illustrate this example, a colleague told me he had a friend who owns a local Chinese lunch restaurant yet could accomplish anything in China.

In hierarchical cultures, this simply doesn't make sense. One would have to seriously question the connections of a man who makes an average sale of $7 for lunch, cooks for a living and has to lock up at night. While this restaurateur was Chinese, it would be impossible for him to be well-connected enough in China to do large-scale, complicated deals.

Don't make the leap that because someone is from a given country, they can do everything you need in that country. Would you hire a Romanian dentist to act as a Romanian negotiator?

RESEARCH OTHER COUNTRIES
BEFORE STARTING THAT BUSINESS TRIP

If you're going to do business with foreign people, you must understand them. All too often, we don't understand who we're dealing with.

When we bring our own mind sets, perceptions, attitudes, values and belief systems to foreign business dealings, we often forget their values and systems are different. Additionally, our foreign counterparts may not be aware of our idiosyncrasies, and may have done little to prepare to meet with us.

Our executives must prepare. Unfortunately, the common argument is that they have busy schedules, hence no time to learn about the places they'll visit.

Conventional wisdom tells us to take courses and hire experts. While this is true, are there things international deal-makers can do right away to increase their understanding?

HERE'S A LIST OF SIMPLE THINGS THAT CAN BE ACCOMPLISHED EVEN BY THE BUSIEST PEOPLE:

- Go to dinner. If your business will take you to Thailand, go to a local Thai restaurant. Try to figure out who the managers and owners are. How are employees treated? How do they behave? Is the food presented in any special way? How long does the meal take, and why? What cultural observations can you draw from the way your meal and payment are handled?

- Read a newspaper from that country. If you can find an English version or are heading to an English-speaking country, this will be easier. But most countries have newspapers that are published on the Internet, and many offer English versions.

Even if the language is different, look at the way the paper is laid out, how ads are handled, what colors (if any) are used and what sections may exist. How sophisticated is the design and typesetting?

- Look up the country in the encyclopedia. Get to know some basic facts about country size, GDP, population, major exports and imports, form of government and religious aspects. Just knowing basic facts will separate you from the many international deal-makers who didn't bother to learn anything.

- Listen to the music. With the Internet and download-able music, one can easily find music from the country they're visiting. And at about $1 per song, it's very affordable to build a quick collection.

Additionally, the Web can steer you to streaming radio stations from countries you visit. Thus, you can listen to Radio Nigeria in your living room.

- Talk to a travel agent. While many of us book tickets online, a travel agent (who has been where you're going) can offer you insights. If the travel agent is a foreigner to that country, like you, they'll be even more valuable. They can share perceptions with you.

- Go to the country's official Web site. See how the host country advertises itself, what it boasts of, what subjects it avoids and how you're advised to prepare. You can also get official information such as weather, visa requirements, currency rates and restrictions.

- Talk to a local. A 10-minutes conversation with someone from the country you're visiting is invaluable. You might ask around to see who knows someone from your destination, or you might chat up the waiter or waitress you'll meet when you have your ethnic meal. If you have an employee from your destination country, invite him/her to lunch.

- Learn some of the language. A few key phrases will give you insight as to how people communicate, whether the language has a masculine and feminine form (like French), how people disagree, inflections, pronunciation and cognates (words that translate directly into English). You might be surprised to see that the Chinese word for sofa is "sha fa" or that the Japanese word for computer is "computer."

- Read a book. Americans are chastised for their lack of historical understanding. Japanese students now out score American students on American history exams. Pick up a book to read on the plane ride over that discusses history, politics or culture.

A fictional novel with some cultural accuracy also will help. James Clavell's novels are an excellent example of this; they all deal with stories in Asia, and educate as well as inform. If you're planning a long stay, the "Culture Shock" series are books written by foreign people who lived where you're going.

- Speak to someone who has been there, done that. If you're sourcing product in Asia, speak to someone who's been involved in those deals, in the same countries you're approaching. If you're marketing in Europe, speak to someone who has marketed products or services in the countries of interest. Find out what went wrong, what went right and what types of obstacles may impede your success.

The few hours spent following this list could reap huge rewards overseas, while avoiding serious pitfalls.

TOP 10 FALSE ASSUMPTIONS IN DOING INTERNATIONAL BUSINESS

We see it repeatedly, from the low-level trainee right up to the CEO. Americans often start with the wrong assumptions when entering a foreign market

The assumption set used when marketing, selling, hiring and buying from foreign countries is critical to our eventual success.

When devising an international strategy for a corporation, the presumptions are the first thing to address.

10. THERE IS AN "INTERNATIONAL MARKET."

Ghana, Greece or Malaysia? This first assumption divides the world into two pieces: us and them. And the danger is apparent: We think of the "rest of the world" as one entity. Intellectually, we know there are several entities, each with their own language, culture and business practices.

9. "BUSINESS IS BUSINESS" (THE WORLD IS GETTING SMALLER).

The shrinking of the planet forces us to make less, not more, suppositions about how our counterparts conduct business. Thirty-five years ago, a $50 million manufacturer didn't worry about Chinese off-shoring, Indian software or Italian design. Today's CEOs must think globally, initially by recognizing the differences, not the similarities.

8. OUR TECHNICAL SKILLS WILL TRANSFER ABROAD.

A CFO is a CFO. An XML programmer is the same anywhere in the world. This attitude costs money, reputation and time to market. The CFO who is an expert in financial modeling needs to interact with locals who may not respect his authority or knowledge, and may organize finances differently.

7. A CONTRACT COMES AT THE END OF THE PROCESS; A DEAL IS A DEAL.

The "holy contract" (as Dutch often call U.S. contracts) comes at the end of U.S. negotiations. Contracts often serve as "outlines" in Southeast Asia, the Middle East, and Central and Eastern Europe. The rule to think about is "first a contract, then a negotiation."

6. DOING INTERNATIONAL BUSINESS IS CHEAP (EVEN FREE).

This assumption is scary. I often speak with CEOs who spend millions of dollars running firms and fighting for market share in their home markets. They then turn around and tell me that "we will take a few business trips, find a partner, and things will succeed abroad. The partner will get the operation profitable, thus there is no need to invest."

One such firm is approaching the largest global market for its service, but the CEO hasn't committed a single dollar. If it costs money to access domestic customers, or get a local factory productive, why would it be free to do the same in China, India or Canada?

5. IF THEY SPEAK LIKE US, THEY THINK LIKE US.

When we deal with Canadians, British, Australians (and even Dutch, Germans and Scandinavians), we conduct business in our mother tongue. But we are also making a leap, assuming their values, goals, beliefs and perceptions match ours. We can speak the same language, but the similarity ends there. The British joke that the United States and Britain are two countries separated by a common language.

4. SUCCESS OVERSEAS DEPENDS ON HOW GOOD OUR PRODUCT OR SERVICE IS.

The better mousetrap isn't the answer. Sales overseas are dependent on having the best relationship. We need to work on our customer intimacy, not our product differentiation.

The United States no longer is the top exporter of technology. We can blame China, or we can wonder why we use CRM software instead of visits to keep track of clients.

3. IMPORTED GOODS ARE OFTEN BETTER.

Evidence of this is that Americans drink French water, drive European cars, wear Italian suits and buy Swiss watches. However, Japanese consumers may be concerned with how Japanese a product is. European firms may wonder about the factories that foreigners will cause to shut down. China makes its own computers and DVD players to stimulate the Chinese industry.

2. MONEY IS THE ULTIMATE REWARD.

Many foreign business people are motivated by status, power and social responsibility. In Poland, it's more prestigious to be a large employer than to be wealthy. The factory boss won't fire his neighbors to make a few extra dollars.

1. THE NO. 1 ASSUMPTION: "IT WORKED IN OUR MARKET. IT SHOULD WORK IN THEIRS."

It would be easy to write an entire column on this assumption.

We sell products in colors that are taboo.

We don't recognize that there may be seven or even 15-steps distribution chains in some markets.

We have firms building to the wrong specifications. For example, we try to sell big refrigerators in countries that use small ones, or attempt to sell autos with steering wheels on the incorrect side. We market milkshakes with no milk in them, labor-saving devices where countries want to keep employment high and sports drinks in countries where there isn't enough food to eat.

So, does your business model make sense for doing business overseas?

'AMERICAN' ISN'T THE INTERNATIONAL LANGUAGE OF BUSINESS

As Americans, we often feel we have a tremendous advantage because our mother tongue is spoken throughout the world. English has now passed Mandarin Chinese as the world's most widely spoken language.

In the United States, we learn English from our parents. However, in much of the world, people learn English in school. When the educational system is good, people learn English well. Conversely in the United States, when our parents and community don't use proper English, neither do we.

Europeans often are amused by the word "ain't." But novelty aside, Americans can be at a disadvantage in international negotiations.

Incorrect grammar, colloquialisms and expressions that don't translate are often our demons in our international dealings.

EXAMPLES:

- "We ran it up the flagpole, but no one saluted."

- "Our point man threw a ballpark figure at our SVP, but she shotgunned that the number was off the wall."

- "There was no way to nail this down."

- "Since there was no front-line person who wanted to upset the applecart, the project went belly up."

Notice the expressions as well as the sports and military terminology. This can serve not only to confuse our foreign counterparts, but also to alienate and offend them.

The United States is a controversial country; the planet has seen our sports heroes misbehave, and our military occupy regions of the world where many think we shouldn't.

Thus, the constant reminder of our military mentality can be quite upsetting to overseas business people. Just recently, the Chinese government referred to the United States as "the country most willing to go to war."

The European joke is, "What do you call someone who speaks three languages? Trilingual. What do you call someone who speaks just one language? American."

American arrogance is a difficult obstacle to overcome. And rather than try to temper it, believe it or not, we actually market it. We are constantly reminding the world that the United States leads the human race in technology adoption.

Incidentally, this marketing point happens to be false. In parts of Europe, people download movies to their cell phones. Chinese send more text messages on cell phones than we do. The Swedish were the first to have their taxicabs accept credit cards. Japanese cell phones soon will have credit card capabilities built into them. German engineers pioneer the best automotive technology. And the list goes on.

American Internet companies continually brag about the United States' e-commerce usage, which is greater than the rest of the world combined

In the e-commerce argument, there's a simple alternative explanation. It's not that we are superior technologically, but more apt culturally to purchase things without any type of relationship or even a personal introduction.

Americans are the only people in the world who do business with strangers.

The best evidence of this is cold calling, which is largely an American phenomenon. Even on a consumer level, we get calls at home from strangers, who often won't even disclose their full names ("I'm Willie, operator No. 10").

These strangers call every night to sell us products that we already have, such as long-distance telephone service or a mortgage. It must work some of the time, or the practice would have stopped by now.

This helps to explain that if an American's current vendor doesn't offer a product she wishes to have (for example, video messaging on her computer) she can simply find another vendor who offers it. A European or Asian counterpart would work with her vendor to find a solution to the problem and perhaps do without the product until it's offered.

Europeans, Asians, Africans and South Americans do business by introduction.

In business, the personal introductions serve as an entry barrier to other vendors, a qualification of the vendor and a built-in troubleshooter (the introducer). The prequalification of being introduced by the correct source is therefore invaluable, and in most countries, a necessity.

Rather than change our entire way of thinking, we can win abroad by simply being sensitive to the fact that others think differently. We need to remember that we may be chosen as suppliers for business partners because of who made the introduction, not because of our pricing or technology.

The United States is lucky to have excellent institutions, a large work force, a free press, an entrepreneurial spirit and laws that help us to succeed. We can live wherever we can afford and leave any time we want. We enjoy the right to criticize our institutions, and improve continuously. But let's not forget our own impediments, one of which is our ethnocentric overconfidence.

Anyone who doubts the point of American arrogance has only to remember this: The United States is the only country in the world that refers to a national sporting event as the "World Series."

ETHICS ARE A SUIT OF CLOTHES

Ethics are a suit of clothes. People who wear blue suits aren't better or worse than people who wear brown suits. They're just different.

The same can be said for sets of ethical actions and beliefs. Everyone likes to believe their suit is white and everyone else's is black. The reality may be that everyone is wearing shades of gray.

An incidental point: White is seen as good in our culture, but Asians associate white with funerals.

Dictionaries define ethics as "the discipline dealing with what is good and bad and with moral duty and obligation." If we're to take that definition as true, then who can possibly say what is moral or immoral? And who can therefore tell us what is ethical?

American business people are always reading about the lack of ethics in places such as China, Russia and Indonesia, to name a few. The articles attribute poor protection of intellectual property, counterfeiting, inaccurate bookkeeping and the continuous requests for bribes as evidence of an ethics vacuum.

In the above countries, it's essential to have strong ties with local government when operating there. The government can act as your partner, shareholder, client – or deal-killer. Americans complain about this. "Why do I need their government as a partner? Why can't I run my business without interference?"

When our government leaders go to China, they confront the Chinese about human rights. Our official policy seems to cast ourselves as the moral leader of the free world, and divide people into two camps: those that are with us and those who aren't.

We do the same thing in business. When our products don't meet local specifications overseas, or our practices won't fit into their protocols, we again wave the ethics stick.

When we travel, we witness the American muscle in penetrating foreign markets, as evidenced by McDonald's or our TV shows. The incorrect leap we then make is that the world wants to be American and thus follow our methodologies.

If we look at the issue of American business practices from abroad, we'll find that many of our practices are seen as quite corrupt.

A FEW PERCEPTION EXAMPLES OF AMERICAN ETHICS:

- Firms take over other firms, and instantly change the business rules and eliminate staff to improve the bottom line.

- We allow ineffective CEOs to exit their firms with golden parachutes.

- When a firm goes bankrupt, the officers usually aren't personally liable and may leave a trail of creditors.

- Women still earn about 70 percent of what men earn.

- Business and politics are represented as separate activities, yet the truth is much different.

- We have taken our highly polluting industries overseas, where the environmental and labor laws are less stringent.

Strict environmental laws are a luxury afforded to the developed nations. Hence, we manufacture where it is easier to pollute.

If the white suit represents good, and the black suit evil, then which suit should we be wearing to that meeting?

If someone is really interested in outside perceptions of American economic practices – both governmental and business – visit Transparency International's Web site (www. transparency.org). This site publishes the corruptions perceptions index (CPI), which rates countries based on perceptions of people who do business in multiple nations. Many will be surprised to learn the United States is ranked

17th, behind such places as Austria (No. 10) and Hong Kong (No. 15). We aren't even in the top 10 percent.

Decker defines corruption as "bending the law to enhance your economic well-being."

If we accept that definition, we must ask: At what levels does corruption exist? As Americans doing business abroad, we tend to see corruption wherever we look. It can exist anywhere, from small to large business, government and academia.

When discussing corruption, South Americans often ask: "Why are you Americans as corrupt as we are, yet you deny it? You do what we do, and then you do worse by not admitting it."

When American cities, counties and states offer tax holidays to lure firms into their region, are they being corrupt? After all, there are already businesses operating, paying taxes and following the rules as they were previously understood. Yet a new firm can come into the market without contributing.

And whatever firms were already established are expected to continue paying taxes, creating jobs, keeping the air clean and staying put. If those established firms looked elsewhere for the same incentives granted to the newcomers, they might be called unethical.

Which suit do you wear to that meeting?

When we discuss ethics with our Asian friends, we often hear the Chinese proverb that reads: "When we have food on the table and clothes on our backs, then we worry about ethics."

But in the United States, we have plenty to eat. How do we justify misconduct?

INTERNATIONAL LICENSING AGREEMENTS: FEAST OR FAMINE

Many firms are using licensing as a tool for market entry, and for good reason.

Take an example of database management software, which may be produced by a firm in the United States. This firm may wish to enter, say, the Japanese market but not have the resources to set up offices, hire local staff, market within Japan and provide the after-sales ongoing service needed by the Japanese clients.

By licensing their technology to a local player, and having the local player take care of local market needs, the U.S. firm can concentrate on supporting the Japanese licensee, and upgrading and augmenting product as needed.

In many cases, the licensee will take care of integration of the foreign technology within their organization. And if there are marketing opportunities beyond the original licensee (a best-case scenario), then the licensee will add staffing, marketing to local clients, sales support and service to their duties.

Foreign producers need to know it's common that the licensee (in this case, the Japanese firm) earns more revenue in Japan than the foreign provider. If the licenser wishes to earn more in foreign markets, it will need more control, which translates to more investment: people, time and money.

Licensing isn't free, however. Aside from the costs in finding the right licensee(s), licensers need to add the costs of teaching, supporting and monitoring to keep the relationship prosperous. The licenser may have to help stimulate local demand for their product. And there are often other costs.

In examining licensing deals, the first thing to decide is whether it's indeed better to license or trade (sell) the product. There are pros and cons of each. Trading gets the seller a single client, and thus the vendor has to keep getting new clients, which is expensive. However, trading can give the vendor more control. The vendor isn't necessarily turning over the entire market to the local client.

Licensing offers lower entry and sustenance costs. And if you manage the licensee correctly, you'll have a local partner who will assist in all the areas mentioned above. However, mismanagement of that relationship can kill a market for a foreign vendor. If the licensee doesn't perform, the vendor may never gain market share in the desired country.

In our Japanese example, U.S. firms typically will engage attorneys to write complicated licensing agreements, demanding "minimum performance guarantees" by the Japanese counterparts.

But what if the Japanese perform up to the contract?

Revoking a license can be difficult in Japan, often impossible. "If everyone knows you are working with Mitsubishi," then it will be assumed you are de facto partners. This means other firms won't be eager to work with you, as they see you're already engaged in a relationship. And if the relationship fails, you may be seen as the one who hasn't performed.

Another negotiator's point in licensing is the type of license. Are you offering exclusivity in the market (meaning no one else can have a license)? Is the license time-sensitive, perhaps valid for one or two years? Is this a license to sell your product, a license to manufacture your product or both?

Are there additional conditions to be placed on the license? For example, who will trademark and (if necessary) patent the product or process you're selling? Will there be any conditions on the type of promotion used? Promotion can include distribution channels, type of media used, pricing and service/guarantee offerings.

How many licenses will be offered in each country/region/ market/industry? Does a license for China include other Chinese-speaking markets? Is your Japanese health care license for health care in Japan only? What industries constitute health care? What about Japanese clients residing outside of Japan?

The locals in their market will want to know what type of investment the suppliers are making. Will they commit funds, technical resources, press visibility, personnel, localization of product (if necessary), localization of marketing materials (if necessary), legal resources in their home market, approval and regulatory fees? Will certain manufacturing standards (such as ISO 9000, Six Sigma) be adhered to? Will the supplier accompany the licensee on sales and service calls, and for what time period?

How is revenue divided? Who holds the pen? Who gets paid first and when are the accounts paid fully? Is the licenser willing to plow back any funds into the local market?

Perhaps the biggest stumbling block is expectations management. Did the U.S. firm do an adequate job of educating the local firm as to its needs? Did the local firm explain issues such as time lines, sales pipelines, finances, negotiation styles and cultural barriers to its new licenser?

I'm always amazed that most licensing negotiations center on protection issues, such as PI, patents, trademarks and repatriation of funds when almost all of those issues are unenforceable.

A thorough discussion (which may take several weeks) of the expectations serves two purposes: It allows the parties to get to know each other better, and it forestalls the cries of "foul" or "nonperformance" because both parties truly understand what type of deal is being created.

THE PHILIPPINES ARE A GOOD ENTRY TO ASIAN MARKETPLACE

What is the best springboard to Asia? Many companies don't bother to debate this question. This is one of the biggest strategic decisions a firm can make, and it's often made quickly, blindly and influenced entirely by emotion. Firms often choose countries on the basis of these variables:

- Someone in the company may have experience in a given area. Perhaps a sales manager may have visited a particular market.

- An employee is a foreign national. It's like deciding to market to Malaysia because a Malaysian engineer works for you.

- Companies follow their clients. While this may be necessary to keep current clients happy, it's an unscientific decision, and gives clients control of a vendor's international strategy.

What happens when clients disappear? Then we have a vendor that has resources in a country it may not otherwise want to invest in.

- Sheer market size. This is tricky; there are different techniques for measuring markets. Are we counting people, money spent or money spent on foreign goods? In some industries, Denmark (5 million population) spends more than China (1.3 billion). Greece eats more cheese per capita than other countries, and outspends Japan on cheese (7 million vs. 135 million people).

- Market potential. "We have to get into China because of the market potential there!" Which market? (Autos, dental supplies, wheat, cooking sherry?) When will that potential be reached? Do we have any reason to believe that while 1 billion people need cooking oil or toilet paper, that these markets could be ours?

- Getting on the bandwagon. Articles in magazines about the wonders of the Indian market alone don't guarantee success when selling into India. Be careful when you read success stories; firms rarely tell reporters about failures.

- Proximity to home market. Market opportunities in adjacent countries seem more attractive and realistic.

- Language compatibility. This is often the main factor for choosing Singapore as the Asian entry port. The language helps, but Singapore is smaller than Chicago in market size and purchasing power.

However, firms might want to sell "country products" to Singapore (aircraft, banking regulatory software, large-scale engineering projects and government lotteries) that Chicago wouldn't be able to buy.

When we look at all of these factors in terms of Asian market entry, companies may do best using the Philippines as a toehold in Asia. There are many reasons for this.

- Proximity to other markets. The Philippines is centrally located in Southeast Asia, often referred to as "the Jewel of the Orient."

- Language compatibility. The official language of the Philippines is English. Certainly, Philippine English will have its inflections and colloquialisms, but it's relatively easy to communicate, especially when compared to China.

- Population size. In 2006, the population of the Philippines is 89 million, with a per-capita income of about $5,100. It's a much better market than Chicago. Compare that with China and Singapore.

- Access to other markets. Because the Philippines is an archipelago, one doesn't drive to other countries. However, market access also can be measured by how well in-country contacts can open up new countries.

It's no secret that much of the Philippine economy is controlled by Filipino Chinese (Filipinos with Chinese genealogy as well) and Chinese-Chinese (100 percent pure Chinese ethnicity) who may have lived in the PI for generations. The "Chinese connection" can make strategic introductions to other Asian markets. Many Chinese families control pan-Asian marketing companies.

- The PI is not a hated country. Often in global business when one country is picked, another (or several others) is alienated. Companies often must choose between India and Pakistan, Japan or China, Taiwan or China (certainly North Korea or the rest of Asia).

The Philippines offers a somewhat neutral meeting and outbound marketing ground. It doesn't own China's controversies, Japan's history or Cambodia's politics.

- Infrastructure in the PI is good. The traffic can be horrendous, but the public systems (electricity, water, air conditioning, sewage) work well.

- The Philippines is a Catholic country. While this may not matter to everyone, it matters to a lot of people. Locals there grew up learning the same super story that Westerners learned: the Bible. Hence, there is an instant overlap with Western Judeo-Christian culture.

Filipinos discuss sin, shared worship and doing good deeds, as Westerners do. The religious practices and the place religion occupies in everyday life are much different than the more religious Indonesia or Thailand.

- Last, the PI is a beautiful place to visit. Foreigners are greeted with some of the world's best cuisine, as well as some of the world's finest hospitality. Sure, there are large, crowded cities, but there are also stunning islands and lush jungles. Road-weary marketers can take a break from traveling constantly throughout Asia, and thus try to host their Asian clients and partners at home. And most Asians will want to visit you there.

SUPPORT FOREIGN DISTRIBUTION

A U.S.-based software firm was attempting to enter Asian markets. It thought the quickest way to success was to find accomplished distributors who would carry its software. U.S. firms experience an 85 percent failure rate selling to Asia, so this firm wasn't willing to undertake heavy investments there

After spending months finding a Singaporean distributor, the firm thought it had gained a foothold in Asia. All the signs were good: Singapore is a technologically advanced, English-speaking market. While its population is only about 3 million, it can be a springboard to the rest of Asia. This distributor was selected because it had many major accounts, and experience selling them foreign software.

The firm learned the Singaporean legal process mirrored the United States' in terms of due diligence, negotiation and contractual obligations.

A year after this distribution partnership was formed, there were no sales. The U.S. firm thought the distributor was lazy. Additionally, the firm thought that since the distributor wasn't keeping its end of the bargain, its partner was unethical.

To start to understand this quagmire, let's see what the expectations were –and what went wrong.

The reality of a distributor not selling aggressively isn't unique to Singapore. This complaint is commonplace throughout Asia and the rest of the world. It's important to understand what distributors do and what they expect.

Think of a distributor as a convenience store. The store may carry many items, but doesn't seem to vigorously sell or market most of them. The store leaves the marketing up to its suppliers. Thus, Coca-Cola will run promotions in convenience stores more often than the store itself will push the soft drink.

The same is true for distributors. It's best to think of them as aiding in logistics more than marketing. There are exceptions to this rule, but usually distributors are driven by their clients.

Once demand for a firm's product is stimulated, good distributors can work well with qualifying prospects, financing, delivery, merchandising and collection. Generally, they leave the marketing to their vendors.

Distributors often have two main questions when they meet with suppliers:

What will you do to stimulate demand (advertising, public relations, direct sales)?

What is my cut?

Researching the market, the promotional tools available and answering these questions satisfactorily will give the partnership the right start. In the United States, a software distributor will have a sales force, but the sellers will have a selection of products to offer. In software, we often refer to these parties as VARs (value added resellers).

The VAR will be interested in how its suppliers will aid in sales.

Will they advertise?

Will they attend sales meetings with them?

Will they train its sales force?

Will they supply relevant, professional marketing materials?

Will key executives be available when needed?

Have they built a strong brand, and are they protecting the brand?

Are they providing any marketing dollars or in-kind contributions (such as company vehicles, cell phones, offices and call center services)?

Obviously, a distribution strategy needs to be well thought out. Add Singapore to the mix, and it gets even more complicated.

In examining our example firm's assumptions, it's wrong to suggest the distributor is "lazy" when much of the above criteria aren't met.

"Unethical" is a term that should never be used in international business. Ethics are a suit of clothes, and your ethics don't equal my ethics, which don't equal Singaporean ethics. The distributor may think the U.S. firm is "unethical" in that it expects to immediately enter a new market and displace long standing vendors.

U.S. firms fail in Asia often because they haven't invested enough. Investment is necessary in, for example, research, market strategy, training of key personnel and distribution support.

Singapore offers several advantages to U.S. firms wishing to lose their innocence in Asia, but in reality, Singapore is very Western. This English-speaking modern market is relatively small, and engages in customs and protocols quite different than those of Japan or even China.

Much of U.S. firms' discussions with the Singaporeans were of a legal nature: minimum sales requirements, margins, product rights, etc. Yet discussions with distributors should be largely focused on client support and marketing. Talking about legal matters was of little help.

While Singapore's technological advantage eases business transactions, it tends to also narrow the United States' technological lead. Singaporean technology works well. The U.S. firm's added value would be greater in a different Asian market.

Last, many firms throughout the world feel that "once distribution is won, the deal is done." In addition to many of the support techniques, it's vital to develop a personal relationship with any Asian business partner. Frequent visits to the distributor and its key clients are necessary.

A solid Asian distribution strategy should encompass continuous support, both on business and personal fronts.

When was the last time you took your distributor to dinner?

TOP 10 MISTAKES MADE IN HIRING FOREIGN NATIONALS

Don't make these errors when you choose who's going to work for you in another country.

1. ASSUME THAT THEY CAN DO ANYTHING AND EVERYTHING REGARDING THEIR COUNTRY.

Too many times, we've seen Chinese engineers acting as negotiators, French diplomats take on the role of market access people, and Taiwanese sales people try to source factories for their employer.

Would we hire an engineer to negotiate in America? Why would we ever do that overseas?

International is an adjective. Being Indian doesn't mean you know everything about India – from production to marketing to advertising to negotiation to dentistry. If we define specific skill sets to accomplish goals in America, why would we lump all the skills into one person for a Hispanic market?

2. ASSUME THAT THEY RESPECT YOUR AUTHORITY.

You may have positional authority (in that you hired them). But in many cultures, true leadership needs to be earned. Your "foreigner" may have more affiliation to a client, market, co-worker or an ex-boss.

In Central and Eastern Europe, entire governments and economies have changed hands because authority was defied. If everyone magically listened to the boss, China wouldn't be the world's factory, and Poland wouldn't be the fastest-growing economy in Central Europe.

3. TREAT THEM AS TRANSLATORS.

Someone who speaks Greek isn't necessarily a Greek translator. And if you have employed Greek managers, then those managers have their own jobs to do and their own agendas in meetings.

Translation is a specialized skill, like sales, accounting or security. If you haven't got a translator when you need one, then you simply haven't invested enough money in your endeavor.

4. TASK THEM AS YOU WOULD AMERICANS.

Today's management styles are about tasking with autonomy, getting "out of the box" and saying things like: "Here's the job, you are the team, make it happen."

But do foreign employees really want to take initiative? Many cultures will be paralyzed by that type of approach, and wait for leadership.

Employees all over the world are people who are tasked, not who are entrepreneurial.

Entrepreneurs leave their employers, start their own businesses and get written about in newspapers. It is uniquely American to have intrapreneurs, that is, entrepreneurs who work within an organization.

5. PICK ONE FOREIGNER TO DO ANOTHER FOREIGNER'S JOB.

This is often seen when a firm hires, for example, a British country manager and tasks him with developing all of Europe. The assumption that "he's European" is an incorrect one. Can he sell in Poland? Is he well-connected in Belgium? Does he speak German? How much does he know about Eastern Europe?

Additionally, country managers often are picked cross-functionally and given marketing, management, sales and production responsibilities. This is a unique and expensive skill mix.

6. ASSUME THEY UNDERSTAND YOU.

Barring language, do they understand the task? Many cultures need to read rather than listen.

Is your language peppered with euphemisms? Are you using jargon they don't know? Are you saying things like "bottom line" or "ASAP" that they won't know?

A tip: Ask your "foreigner" to write down a description of what you've just asked her to do. See if her description matches your wishes. It will take some extra time, but how much time will a misunderstanding take?

7. ASSUME THEY'LL TELL YOU WHEN THEY DON'T UNDERSTAND.

In one example, a Russian subsidiary was sent boxes of new software to install on company computers. It never happened, as the Russians never were taught how to do it.

They waited for leadership, as good employees would. And rather than communicate their lack of skills, which would be embarrassing, they assumed headquarters would find out and fix the problem.

8. ASSUME THEY WILL TRAIN YOU.

It's a confrontational, risk-taking endeavor to turn to your boss and tell her she's wrong. Most American employees don't have the courage to do this.

How can we expect an immigrant – hoping for the American dream, trying her best in a foreign culture and living with frequent misunderstandings – to confront and correct her boss, even if that's written into her job description?

There are Chinese employees in Asia who don't even know their own salaries until they start work. If they can't negotiate salary with their bosses, they sure won't correct us on our faux pas.

9. MAKE NO EFFORT TO BE FRIENDS.

Business is personal. The thought that work friends are different from other friends is unusual for many cultures.

Once confronted with American systems of segregating relationships, "foreigners" may not approach you to socialize. In almost any country, the boss and co-workers would look after their "foreign guests." Dinner invitations, holiday celebrations, and questions about home, family and hobbies would be commonplace.

10. ASSUME THEY WORK FOR YOU.

This is particularly worrisome when employing someone abroad. They may carry your card and cash your paycheck, but who are they working for? What are their affiliations?

The best advice is to hire slowly. Get to know the person you're hiring and their motivations.

DOING BUSINESS IN CHINA, INDIA REQUIRES A LOT OF GIVE AND TAKE

It's clear to most international business people that the future of global trade greatly depends on what happens with the two Asian powerhouses, China and India.

When U.S. companies look at China and India, they see millions of potential customers, international off-shoring possibilities and formidable competitors.

The numbers are compelling.

India ranks as the 20th-largest purchaser of Colorado goods, while China ranks fourth. China's GDP will rival that of all of Western Europe by 2015.

The middle class of each country is expected to hit 500 million people by 2012. This suggests a potential consumer market of 1 billion people. Blinded by the possibility of increased dollars, yen or Euros, marketers eagerly look for any possible way to gain entry into these countries.

While China and India represent large markets, they also are essential proving grounds for other overseas expansion. If you can do business in China and India, you can do business anywhere.

When companies start to add the low cost of labor in these countries to the proximity to emerging consumer markets, it's easy to see why they want to do business there.

However, many marketers are getting bloodied on the front line. We can't just take a plane ride, open up our briefcases and sell to these countries. It takes time and an enormous amount of effort.

A great way to test a U.S. firm's intentions is to gauge its investments – financial and otherwise. What language is it speaking – English or the local language? Did the company buy an apartment or do executives stay in a hotel? Has it localized marketing materials, products and pitches? Do executives stay for three days or three weeks?

Beyond the basic investments needed for any overseas market, China and India simply aren't easy countries in which to do business. We know that in all business situations, there must be mutual, and usually multiple, benefits.

However, many American and European companies are concerned that the concessions extracted by China and India are highly unusual and burdensome, and leave those businesses vulnerable.

For example, when Boeing wanted to sell aircraft to China's government, it was necessary to have some of the aircraft designed and built in China by Chinese workers. Throughout China, firms often encounter rules that require local labor to be used.

In order for mobile telephone carriers to gain access to India, they had to reveal their secret technologies, management styles and methodology to the Indian government. Whenever possible, India insists on using locally made components, having a hand in the R&D process and serving in board seats of foreign companies operating there.

Offsets frequently are utilized to keep the trade balance in line. An offset is when a U.S. company sells product into India but then is required to purchase a certain amount of Indian product in return. Sometimes offsets can refer to the labor, machines, hardware, software or intelligence required for the project.

Recently, a European food-processing firm entering China was required to hire 50 percent Chinese management (thus necessitating training them), 100 percent Chinese engineers, 100 percent Chinese labor, build the factory with Chinese construction materials and submit blueprints to the Chinese patent offices for the proprietary technology that was being imported into China.

The European company eagerly agreed to all the concessions. Though the average pay is still under $80 per month in China, the European company still thought the market potential was huge enough to justify its concessions.

If you wish to have access to these markets, you need something to give. It can be money, technology, jobs, intelligence or new skills.

The ultimate challenge then would be how can we give to gain access while still protecting ourselves? If we hand over too much IP, won't our customers come back as competitors?

There's good news, however. The most sought-after commodity we can give is intelligence.

China and India covet our business intelligence, sales competence, marketing savvy, modern management techniques, data in worker productivity, environmental clean-up techniques and entrepreneurial creativity.

And the better news is that we're already selling it, as well as giving it away. Anyone who registers with one of our universities, reads our management texts, subscribes to our business papers or surfs our Web sites can gain this know-how. So, in fact, we're being asked for what we are already prepared to part with.

The smart negotiator will try to sell it, not just give it away.

LOCALS DEVISE INGENIOUS SOLUTIONS, AID U.S. FIRMS

When you have a Russian problem, you need a Russian solution.

Americans often refer to themselves as great entrepreneurs and innovators. U.S. companies tend to outspend almost every other country on research and development, and American CEOs often refer to themselves as "chief visionaries."

Yet, the great American ingenuity often pales in significance to the creative problem-solvers we meet in foreign markets.

In one instance, a large U.S. mining firm was setting up offices in Rumania. It encountered enormous stumbling blocks.

The first problem came from the local telephone company. It needed several cumbersome documents to be filled out in triplicate, and there was a six-month waiting period to get telephone services established. This was before the days of GSM cell phones, where one could simply use American, French or Dutch phones.

Consultants suggested solutions such as handing out equity in their firm, employing a government official on retainer, bribes, gifts and seeking justice in the Rumanian courts.

The research office it was establishing sat in a primarily residential apartment building, as the "office" was really just a converted apartment.

As the Americans were figuring out how to break the news to headquarters, one of the Rumanian local hires came up with an instant solution. He suggested they contact their residential neighbors and ask if a phone line could be strung from their apartments – so the firm could use the phones during the day, when the phone owners were at work.

Naturally, they would pay for this service. And the payment that was agreed to was more than these apartment dwellers were earning each month. As you can imagine, the neighbors were lined up to help out.

So the phone company's long lead time was much less harmful than had been predicted.

Another time, while touring a Russian LPG (liquid petroleum gas) company near St. Petersburg, we noticed a warehouse full of tractor tires and engine parts. Since none of these were used in the filling or distributing of LPG tanks, we had to question the need for this equipment.

We were told these parts were hard to obtain east of Saint Petersburg. Thus they were a valuable commodity that could be used to trade for gasoline, fresh water and safety equipment (all goods the LPG company had trouble buying on the open market). Again, this was a local solution that made complete sense.

Americans often refer to themselves as great entrepreneurs and innovators. U.S. companies tend to outspend almost every other country on research and development, and American CEOs often refer to themselves as "chief visionaries."

Yet, the great American ingenuity often pales in significance to the creative problem-solvers we meet in foreign markets.

In one instance, a large U.S. mining firm was setting up offices in Rumania. It encountered enormous stumbling blocks.

The first problem came from the local telephone company. It needed several cumbersome documents to be filled out in triplicate, and there was a six-month waiting period to get telephone services established. This was before the days of GSM cell phones, where one could simply use American, French or Dutch phones.

Consultants suggested solutions such as handing out equity in their firm, employing a government official on retainer, bribes, gifts and seeking justice in the Rumanian courts.

The research office it was establishing sat in a primarily residential apartment building, as the "office" was really just a converted apartment.

As the Americans were figuring out how to break the news to headquarters, one of the Rumanian local hires came up with an instant solution. He suggested they contact their residential neighbors and ask if a phone line could be strung from their apartments – so the firm could use the phones during the day, when the phone owners were at work.

Naturally, they would pay for this service. And the payment that was agreed to was more than these apartment dwellers were earning each month. As you can imagine, the neighbors were lined up to help out.

So the phone company's long lead time was much less harmful than had been predicted.

Another time, while touring a Russian LPG (liquid petroleum gas) company near St. Petersburg, we noticed a warehouse full of tractor tires and engine parts. Since none of these were used in the filling or distributing of LPG tanks, we had to question the need for this equipment.

We were told these parts were hard to obtain east of Saint Petersburg. Thus they were a valuable commodity that could be used to trade for gasoline, fresh water and safety equipment (all goods the LPG company had trouble buying on the open market). Again, this was a local solution that made complete sense.

However, this particular Russian was well-connected with local government officials and our Russian clients. There would be no way to maintain business continuity if we replaced him with another manager. It seemed we were stuck with him.

Therefore, the only solution was to bring in a strong, Western-trained manager to serve as his director of operations. As chief operation officer, this new manager would have signing authority on deals and be responsible to keep headquarters informed. Additionally, his Western training enabled him to communicate the nuances about the Russians to our firm, and vice versa.

Too often we look at a foreign work practice, see perceived injustices within it and try to make changes.

When acquiring a factory in Indonesia, the European buyers thought the first thing they would do is motivate their lackadaisical workers by changing their pay scales. This seemed to be a natural win-win situation. The staff would double their earnings from $1 to $2 per day. The firm would get its first choice of new hires drawn by higher wages, a much more loyal work force, positive local press and high moral praise back home.

The end result of this plan surprised everyone. When the first Friday payday rolled around, there didn't seem to be much rejoicing by the employees. The staff received their paychecks rather nonchalantly. They took their pay home. The next Monday, the work force was gone.

While the European management was stumped, some Indonesian management was dispatched to the workers' homes.

After some research, the firm learned the workers thought they were being paid to take off an additional week (as they had enough money to live for two weeks now) and would return in one week's time expecting their jobs back.

The Europeans weren't able to change the local "living paycheck to paycheck" culture. And the Indonesians were more motivated to enjoy their time instead of accumulating wealth.

Learning local motivations would be the Indonesian solution to an Indonesian problem.

POLAND IS A GOOD COUNTRY IN WHICH TO DO BUSINESS

Before you try to break into the Chinese market, have you considered Poland? We tend to see massive coverage about China and India, but are there easier places to do business?

How can we tell if Poland is a market worth entering?

Let's look at some criteria that will help grade the country.

- Geography – Poland borders seven countries: Germany, the Czech Republic, Slovakia, Ukraine, Byelorussia,

Russia (a small section known as Kaliningrad) and Lithuania. That's seven countries within driving distance.

Poland is in the middle of Europe, putting it the unique position of being a crossroads, a stop-off point and a springboard to European nations. On its northern side, Poland is bordered by the Baltic Sea, allowing for direct ocean cargo in and out of the country.

- Facts and figures – Poland's $514 billion GDP is growing at an estimated 3.2 percent per year, according the CIA world fact book (www.cia.gov/cia/publications/factbook).

The Web site also indicates 10.6 million Internet users and a labor force of 17 million from Poland's population of 38.5 million. While the corruption perception index (corruption rated by business people) places Poland in 70th place, China is still behind at 78th. India is ranked at 88th (www.transparency.org).

Hence, Poland still is trying to organize its market. Many firms dealing with regulation, financial reporting, negotiation training, security and public relations are finding market opportunities in Poland. Smart firms get retainers.

- The European Union – Poland joined the EU in 2004. This forces higher standards in government, law, banking and commerce, and removes trade barriers among EU countries. Poland can offer a cornerstone in a 25-country market, comprising 450 million people.

Because Poland doesn't possess the great wealth found in the UK, Germany or France, it receives EU grants, soft loans and other aid. Firms that know how to procure these donor funds from the organizations that offer them (for example, World Bank, Eureka and IMF) will be in advantageous positions, providing the funds are used to enhance Poland's infrastructure.

- Infrastructure – Poland has many of the amenities that foreign business people require, such as clean hotels, an extensive network of ground transportation, Internet capabilities, telephones, modern banks, and of course, dining and entertainment.

Its infrastructure still is being upgraded, with help from EU funds. This is obviously a market opportunity for those who can design and build roadways, railways, telecommunications networks, environmental cleanup facilities, office parks and airports.

- Culture – Poles tend to express their feelings openly, have a strong work ethic and believe they can chart their own futures.

Because Poland is a socialist country, groups are important identifiers in its society. Negotiations are more commonly performed in teams, and while consensus isn't always reached, it's sought. This is in stark contrast to the American way of working, the individualistic nature of our society and the belief that "the buck stops here."

When selling within Poland, relationships are essential, and appropriate introductions can make or break any deal. Again, this contrasts the American "business is business" mentality, where we can sign deals with total strangers and expect the law to protect us. Customer intimacy is what assures smooth transactions in Poland.

Women can transact business in Poland. While the role of women doesn't equal the Scandinavians', women's rights far surpass those in China or India.

- American-friendly – There are an estimated 27 million Americans with at least some Polish ancestry. The largest Polish city is Warsaw, with 2.2 million people. The city with the second-largest Polish population is Chicago.

Poland has been pro-American for decades, and has supported the United States militarily and politically. American media can be found on TV, radio, digitally and in movie theaters. Poles will try to speak English with Americans, and many will have some knowledge of our culture or history.

- Springboard to elsewhere – Because of Poland's location, its similarity to other Slavic nations and the entrepreneurial spirit of the Poles, the country makes an excellent springboard to other nations.

Having a Polish headquarters may not carry any caché in Paris, Madrid or London, but Warsaw is the smart location for points south and east. Many Eastern Europeans look up to the Poles as pioneers in government and business.

Shrewd firms place their European headquarters in a prestigious Western European city and use Warsaw as their base when dealing with the CIS (Commonwealth of Independent States, the former USSR countries) or the Baltic nations of Latvia, Lithuania and Estonia.

- Hospitality – Perhaps the most compelling reason to do business in Poland is the Polish sense of hospitality. Poles view business people as guests who need help in their country. Poles will go out of their way to offer help to the lost, food to the hungry or advice to the curious. Poles love humor and enjoy new people.

20 KEYS TO SUCCESS IN INTERNATIONAL MARKETS

"Plan your work, and work your plan." An international market entry plan contains hundreds of elements, but these initial 20 are the most critical for success abroad:

1. AN APPROPRIATE AMOUNT OF PLANNING TIME.

Too often companies approach foreign markets and cut corners on the necessary planning time. Executives will not dedicate their time, hire the correct resources, and spend the money to plan a proper market entry strategy. The idea of "getting on a plane and getting a deal" simply does not work overseas.

2. AN ACTIONABLE GOAL.

A goal is a number (think of hockey goals). The goals can be sales volume, number of accounts, market share, points on customer satisfaction surveys, margin, profit, ROI, or whatever benchmarks the firm uses. Frequently markets are approached without goals that can be articulated within and outside the company.

3. A REALISTIC OBJECTIVE.

Objectives refer to the situation the company wishes to be in, usually in regards to market position. For example, are you the low-cost supplier? Are you the market leader? Are you associated with a luxury position in the market? Are you the convenient choice? Are you aiming for profit or market share?

4. A LOGICAL MARKET SCREENING MECHANISM.

Buzzwords like "China's 1.5 billion people" or "Denmark's 4.2 million citizens" point to a laziness when defining which markets to approach. A matrix that makes sense to your organization needs to be employed.

5. A TRUE UNDERSTANDING OF THE MARKET CONDITIONS.

How is the how the market organized? How does distribution work? What are the price points? Who are the major players?

6. A REGULATORY STRATEGY.

Where will foreign governments help you and where will they block your progress? Are you in touch with local leaders when necessary? And will your government allow you to sell in a foreign market? Are there any conditions you must satisfy to be able to do this?

7. A COMPETITIVE ANALYSIS.

Who are you displacing by being in the market? Who will try to block your presence there? What advantages do you have over your new competitors? What is their competitive advantage, and how will you overcome it? What are your rivals doing to price, promote, distribute, and enhance product?

8. A TRUE UNDERSTANDING OF THE CUSTOMER.

What are the customers' buying habits? Who are the customer groups? How will you approach the clientele? What is the sales cycle like in this country? What motivates the client to buy? Are customers open to the idea of new players in the market?

9. A GENUINE "MODE OF ENTRY" STRATEGY.

What will be your way in to this market? What kind of support will your salespeople need? Will you be selling directly or through some form of distribution? Are there other firms you can cooperate with to gain market entry?

10. REALISTIC EXPECTATIONS.

Has your firm been educated in how long and how difficult this market will be to enter? As each market has specific and varying conditions, each territory must be carefully studied.

11. THE CORRECT MARKET CHAMPIONS.

Companies can often leap to the conclusion that success at home will equal success abroad. The one liner: "Jim Bob did such a good job selling in Kansas, we're giving him Tokyo."

12. CROSS CULTURAL AND COUNTRY TRAINING.

Does your staff understand the nuances of doing business in the particular countries you have chosen? Are you training them continuously?

13. A "ROADBLOCK" MAP.

What impediments exist to your success? Cultural, legal, political, infrastructure, personnel, or funding?

14. INTEREST IN MORE THAN THE MONEY.

Do the people involved really enjoy the country in question? Are they invested personally in learning some language, the customs, the food, the entertainment? If an executive loves India, he/she will have a higher probability of success than someone who merely tolerates it.

15. FEEDBACK ON MARKET CONDITIONS.

Do you have a mechanism to gather and disseminate information on the market? Will the knowledge be utilized?

16. A BUDGET THAT MAKES SENSE.

Only after goals and objectives are set, and market knowledge is gathered and understood, should a budget be prepared. We continuously see the opposite approach of "let's throw X dollars at the market."

17. EXECUTIVE INVESTMENT.

Not a budget, but an investment in time and effort. The CEO who flies to Paris for a two day meeting is basically telling the French: "I don't care about you; I just want your money."

18. HUMILITY.

When we play in someone else's sandbox, we need to remember we don't set the rules, they do.

19. PATIENCE.

With the main cultural difference being how time is viewed, we can bet that our international counterparts will take longer to make and implement decisions than we do in the USA.

13 MISTAKES MADE WHEN DEALING WITH CHINESE

ASSUMING ALL CHINESE ARE ALIKE

Singapore Chinese resemble mainland Chinese the way Americans resemble British. Shared language, some shared values, but otherwise different business techniques and norms

MOVING TOO QUICKLY; NOT HAVING ENOUGH TIME

Chinese cultures are ancient. China is the last of the great civilizations, with a 4000+ year history. They are patient. And the one who is most impatient has the disadvantage

Americans in particular are notorious for planning trips that are too short

THINKING "YES" MEANS "YES"

"Yes" may mean: "I've heard you" or "I understand." There are no words for "yes" and "no" in the Chinese language. Finite concepts like that are foreign to them.

THINKING "A DEAL IS A DEAL"

The Mainland Chinese philosophy is that one can always negotiate. Thus, signed contracts are easily and often re-negotiated.

DOING BUSINESS WITH STRANGERS

In other words, being task oriented in a relationship oriented environment. Business is done through introduction, and by relationship

USING THE LAW AS A SHIELD

Relationships serve to protect the parties. An MOU is preferable to a contract in most cases. And if you choose to use the law to protect you, which laws will you use, and where will you enforce?

REFUSING CHINESE HOSPITALITY

When Chinese offer to host a banquet, buy you lunch or dinner, they mean it! Chinese hospitality is second to none, and outsiders are received as guests in their country.

NOT UNDERSTANDING CULTURAL NORMS: BUSINESS CARDS, GREETING, INTRODUCTIONS

Naturally, training is available. "Business is Business" is a fallacy. And Westerners can be so successful in their home countries; they forget they are just beginners in China

SPEAKING OF BUSINESS TOO QUICKLY

This speaks again of the relationship aspect to business negotiations. First the relationship, then the business discussions

VIEWING MAINLAND CHINA AS ONE MARKET

Besides various regional differences, China has political elite, an entrepreneurial powerhouse class, a growing middle class, and over a billion other people who want more to eat.

USING THE WRONG CHINESE IN THE WRONG MARKET

Looking Chinese and speaking Chinese are not enough. Political and business contacts are essential to get things done in China. Classic blunders have occurred when overseas Chinese were hired to establish businesses in Mainland China, but they didn't have the clout to get to right people. Look for strong connections more than skin color

ASKING A CHINESE SECRETARY IN YOUR OFFICE TO ACT AS A TRANSLATOR

Is your Chinese secretary a professional interpreter? Language skills alone do not make for an interpreter.

USING THE WRONG NEGOTIATORS

How many times have I heard: We have someone in our office from China, he'll negotiate with our Chinese counterparts? The head waiter of the Los Angeles Hyatt speaks Chinese too. Would you have him negotiate for you? It is essential to use professional negotiators who

a) Understand your business and

b) Understand China and Chinese business and

c) Are able to be positioned correctly in Chinese hierarchies.

This article was provided for your information. Drop us a line if we can be of any help in:

- Gaining market access in China (or elsewhere)

- Professional negotiation services

- Training your existing staff in what to expect abroad

10 COMMON MISTAKES MADE WHEN DEALING WITH INDIA

10. THE EXPECTATION THAT A CONTRACT ENDS THE NEGOTIATION.

Many times, a contract is singed, and then negotiations continue. Business people in India do not place the contract at the end of an agreement.

9. THE ASSUMPTION THAT INDIA IS HOMOGENOUS.

India is old, and large. It has geographic, cultural, and religious differences just as any large country does.

8. THE LACK OF PATIENCE.

India does not put the same emphasis in time as we in the west do, particularly the USA.

7. WHEN OUTSOURCING, FIRMS PUT TECHNICAL EXPERTS IN CHARGE OF INDIA PROJECTS.

Are your technical experts negotiators? Are they cross cultural specialists? If they possess both of those characteristics in addition to their technical expertise, then use them. Otherwise, supplement them with your business people

6. LACK OF TRAINING ON THE INDIA TEAM.

"Software is software, leather jackets are leather jackets. If we know the business, we can work internationally." This is simply NOT TRUE! Your staff dealing with India needs to be trained in HOW to conduct business there.

5. LACK OF SUPPORT FOR INDIA'S DISTRIBUTORS AND PARTNERS.

This mistake is made throughout the planet, including the home country of various firms. Distributors need partners that will stimulate sales, and help them sell within their markets. Otherwise, sales will be disappointing.

4. ASSUMPTIONS MADE REGARDING LOCAL LAWS, AND HOW TO ENFORCE THEM.

India is not a litigious country. Therefore, it is necessary to figure out how to solve problems non-confrontationally.

3. THE USE OF WESTERN PROJECT MANAGEMENT SKILLS TO MANAGE INDIAN WORKERS.

Again, Gant charts, MBO timetables, and artificial deadlines alone aren't sufficient. And usually, the Asians will want many people involved, not just a Project Manager. They will also expect you to spend time developing a working relationship, which is often personally based.

2. THE ASSUMPTION THAT OUTSOURCING TO INDIA WILL BRING IMMEDIATE SAVINGS.

This is usually untrue. There are set up costs, delays, and a relationship building process that will eat up much of the savings expected in the first year or two.

1. THE ASSUMPTION THAT "IF THEY SPEAK ENGLISH, THEY MUST THINK LIKE US"

Nothing can be farther from the truth. Americans are typically poor at realizing that cultural biases are largely invisible. English ability does not guarantee similar thought, ethics, customs, or negotiation points.

This article was provided for your information. Drop us a line if we can be of any help in:

- Gaining market access in India (or elsewhere)

- Professional negotiation services

- Training your existing staff in what to expect abroad

TEN TIPS FOR BETTER STRATEGIC PLANNING

The words "entrepreneur" and "shoot from the hip" often

go hand in hand. But as the pace of business increases at an ever-accelerating rate, so does the need for planning.

In many industries, the barriers to entry have been dramatically reduced. Competitors can come in from way out in left field and put you out of business with ideas you never thought of. Planning forces you to pay attention to what is going on in the world so you can avoid that fate.

Many entrepreneurs avoid strategic planning because they consider it a highly complex process that costs a lot of money and saps the time and energy of the senior management team. But strategic planning doesn't have to be mysterious, complicated or time-consuming. In fact, for entrepreneurial companies, it ought to be quick, simple and easily implement-able."

To get the most out of your strategic planning process, here are 10 tips:

Gather a representative team. Bring together a small team (six to ten people) of company leaders and managers who represent every area of the company.

Go off-site. To minimize distractions and maximize focus, conduct your strategic planning session away from the office. A well-run strategic planning retreat should take two days, three at the most.

Get full commitment from your management team. You can't do it alone. If your management team doesn't buy into the plan, it won't happen.

Let go of the reins. The CEO should not lead the planning retreat. When you do, people wonder whether you are trying to lead them down the path you wanted all along. Participate actively, but don't dominate the session.

Use an objective third-party facilitator. To lead the session, hire a trained professional who has no emotional investment in the outcome of the plan. An impartial third party can concentrate on the process rather than the end result and ask the tough questions that others might fear to ask.

Include an action plan. To have any chance at implementation, the plan must clearly articulate goals, action steps, responsibilities, accountabilities and specific deadlines. The action plan should also state that the strategic plan is the beginning of implementation.

Don't use indelible ink. Good strategic plans are fluid, not rigid and unbending. They allow you to adapt to changes in the marketplace. Your goals won't change very often, but your action steps will.

Don't let the facilitator write the plan. The team should write the plan during the meeting. The facilitator merely serves as the tour guide.

Get commitment in writing. Before closing the strategic planning session, have team members pledge their commitment in writing to the plan and its successful execution. When you walk out of the room everyone must fully support the plan – even though they may not agree with everything in it.

Review the plan regularly. Review the strategic plan for performance achievement no less than quarterly and as often as monthly or weekly. Focus on accountability for results and have clear and compelling consequences for unapproved missed deadlines.

Refer to the Chapter ***Market Entry Pathways*** for more information

Introduction to the Market Access Screen

To download and use the market access screen, please visit

www.marketaccessscreen.com

So, how do we really compare one market to another? There are many variables in deciding which country (and which region within a given country) is the right place to do business.

Many firms go into new markets with very little knowledge as to whether that market is the right fit. We often hear terms such as "market size" and "purchasing power" as cornerstones of a strategy. The Market Access Screen goes into some 80 or 90 different variables, including: cultural fit, the ability to move money freely, a transparent legal system, necessary infrastructure and the amount of product modification required. There are many other issues to consider and your own firm may have very unique conditions or constraints to consider.

Finally, there is some methodology available! The Market Access Screen was created after engaging in hundreds of international market entry deals…the need for a tool such as this one was apparent.

This proprietary tool was built to help firms compare and contrast overseas markets with some real criteria. This grading system will help a firm use objective data to really draw out the pros and cons of different markets. At the end of the exercise, users will have a raw score that they can use to back up their decisions. The Market Access Screen is a living document; one must be able to manipulate and modify it. It is available to you for free under the "additional resources" section. Because the Market Access Screen is a spreadsheet, it is automatically in a format that business people will understand quickly. The data as well as the presentation can be completely customized.

Included with the Market Access Screen is an audio presentation, which explains each entry and helps guide the user through the process.

THE MARKET ACCESS SCREEN

Audio for this section is at marketentrytoolkit.com**. Click on "Readers."**

Criteria		Weight	Raw Score (-5 to +5)	Total
				Country A
Market Questions				
Market size		3		
Expressed market need		3		
Contacts (do you have them)		10		
Approachability (getting to the M.A.N.)		2		
Anticipated success for high margin		2		

Criteria		Weight	Raw Score (-5 to +5)	Total
Cultural Questions				
(Understanding theirs. More need lower #)	religious background	2		
	local language needed?	2		
	mgmt styles compatible	2		
(Longer term orientation, lower the #)	time	2		

149

Criteria		Weight	Raw Score (-5 to +5)	Total
Lower # if rtsp needed; don't have it)	task/ relationship	2		
(The more collective, lower the #)	individual/ collective	1		
(More context oriented, lower #)	context culture h/l	1		

Criteria		Weight	Raw Score (-5 to +5)	Total
Market environment questions				
Political understanding necessary?	(more need, lower #)	2		
Current market presence		3		
Us blocked from selling to them	(the more, the lower the #)	deal killer?		
Anti us sentiment		3		
Competitive questions				
	"taken/ available" market	3		
	5w's answerable	3		
(if there is, lower #)	strong/required local player	2		
	competitive analysis ability	3		
(No p risk is 5)	political risk	2		
Amount/infrastructure you invest		2		

Criteria		Weight	Raw Score (-5 to +5)	Total
Availability of supplier services		2		
Availability of incidental services		2		
Transparency	culture			
	business	1		
	legal	2		
	what do they regard as truth	2		
	culture	1		
(Do you know what…)	business			

Criteria		Weight	Raw Score (-5 to +5)	Total
Client questions		**2**		
Offset requirements (if low positive number)		3		
Do they have money?		2		
Are they a good credit risk?		2		
Ethical match				
Buying habits		2		
(Do you understand)	decision processes	2		
(Do you know)	client concerns	2		
(Do you know)	need	3		
(Do you know)	motivations	2		
Access to our firm (easy to get to us)		1		

Criteria		Weight	Raw Score (-5 to +5)	Total
Legal battlefield (is it a?)		3		
Will they need special terms?		1		
Leverage to other opportunities		2		
	in country	1		
	out of country	2		

Criteria		Weight	Raw Score (-5 to +5)	Total
Operational costs				
(High invest is neg. Number)	inward investment	3		
(More localization more negative)	product localization	1		
Local representation		1		
Legal restrictions				
(If process easy, positive #)	licenses/ permits	2		
(If process easy, positive #)	imports	3		
(Less required, higher #)	% local labor	2		
(Difficulty, more difficult is neg)	labor laws	3		
(The more needed, the lower #)	local content in product	2		

Criteria		Weight	Raw Score (-5 to +5)	Total
Modification questions				
(Less modifying, higher number)	product	3		
(Less modifying, higher number)	service	3		
Marketing				
(Less change, higher number)	how	3		
	materials	2		
(Less modifying, higher number)	delivery	2		
(Less modifying, higher number)	translation	2		
Sales				
(Less change, higher number)	methods	2		
(Shorter term, higher number)	time	2		

Criteria		Weight	Raw Score (-5 to +5)	Total
Cost of Sale				
(your cost to sell, high is lower #)				
Assuming no direct client history, not bound to certain clients, competitive product	operations (transaction)	3		
Neg 3 worst case, 3 best case, 0 neutral/don't know		3		

Audio: How to Use Market Access Screen

You may access the following audio files at: <u>marketentry-toolkit.com/welcome/readers</u>

11. HOUSEKEEPING

12. HOUSEKEEPING2

13. INTRO

14. SCREEN EXPLANATION 15. MARKET SIZE

16. EXPRESSED MARKET NEED 17. CONTACTS

18. APPROACHABILITY

19 .MARKET QUESTIONS

20. CULTURAL QUESITONS R L M 21. TIME

22. RELATIONSHIP TASK

23. COLLECTIVE INDIVIDUAL

24. CONTEXT CONTENT

25. POLITICAL UNDERSTANDING 26. MARKET PRESENCE

27. US BLOCKED

28. ANTI US SENTIMENT

29. TAKEN AVAILABLE

30. 5 W'S

31. LOCAL PLAYER

32. COMP ANALYSIS

33. POLITICAL RISK

34. INFRASTRUCTURE

35. SUPPLIER SERVICES

36. INCIDENTAL SERVICES

37. TRANSPARENCY CULTURE BUS LEGAL

38. TRUTH

39. CLIENT QUESTIONS

40. OFFSET

41. MONEY

42. CREDIT RISK

43. ETHICAL MATCH

44. BUYING HABITS

45. BUYING HABITS

46. LEGAL BATTLEFIELD

47. SPECIAL TERMS

48. LEVERAGE TO OTHER OPPS

49. INWARD INVESTMENT

50. LOCALISATION

51. LOCAL REPS

The Licensing Checklist

INTERNATIONAL LICENSING AGREEMENTS POINTS AND QUESTIONS

1) TRADE VS. LICENSE

- Do you try to sell product, or license your technology or brand?

2) TYPE OF LICENSE

- Exclusivity
- Duration
- Conditions
- Manufacturing
- Media/marketing procedures
- Trademarks and other IP
- Code/parts/portions

3) # LICENSE PER COUNTRY/REGION/MARKET/INDUSTRY

4) INVESTMENT BY MANUFACTURER

- Money
- Technical resources
- Press Visibility

- Personnel
- Legal resources in home market
- Approval/legal fees overseas
- Travel & Expenses
- Facilitation payment
- Marketing budget
- Translation of printed material
- Web Presence (localized)
- Office (in home market and abroad)
- Manufacturing standardization (ISO 9000, etc.)/Compliance

5) REPUTATION OF FIRM IN HOME MARKET

- Press
- Marketing material
- Key staff

6) EXPECTATIONS MANAGEMENT

- Timeline
- Finances
- Negotiation Style
- Cultural barriers

7) INVESTMENT BY LICENSEE

- Funding
- Staff
- Executive time
- Planning
- Marketing plan
- Marketing expenses
- Brochures
- Catalogs
- Samples/Demos
- Website/SEO
- Sales plan
- Operations plan
- Collection
- Supervision
- Reporting

8) REMUNERATION

- "Hold the pen"
- How much and when

9) PROTECTION

- IP
- Patents
- Trademarks
- Enforcement

WHAT SHOULD BE IN ANY MARKETING PLAN
(Whether It Is International Or Domestic)

NAME OF PRODUCT-MARKET

- Major screening criteria relevant to product-market opportunity selected

- Quantitative (ROI, profitability, risk level, etc.)

- Qualitative (nature of business preferred, social responsibility, etc.)

- Major Constraints

CUSTOMER ANALYSIS
(ORGANIZATIONAL OR FINAL CUSTOMER)

- Possible segmenting dimensions (customer needs, other characteristics)

- Identification of qualifying dimensions and determining dimensions

- Identification of target market(s) (one or more specific segments)

- Operational characteristics (demographics, geographic locations, etc.)

- Potential size (number of people, dollar purchase potential, etc.) and likely growth

- Key psychological and social influences on buying purchase

- Type of buying situation

- Nature of relationship with customer

COMPETITOR ANALYSIS

- Nature of current/likely competition

- Current and prospective competitors (and/or rivals)

- Current strategies and likely response to plan

- Competitive barriers to overcome and sources of potential competitive strategy

ANALYSIS OF OTHER ASPECTS OF EXTERNAL MARKET ENVIRONMENT (FAVORABLE AND UNFAVORABLE FACTORS AND TRENDS)

- Economic environment

- Technological environment

- Political and legal environment

- Cultural and social environment

COMPANY ANALYSIS

- Company objectives and overall marketing objectives

- Company resources

- S.W.O.T.T: Identification of major strengths, weaknesses, opportunities, threats & trends (based on above analysis of company resources, customers, competitors and other aspects of external market environment)

MARKETING INFORMATION REQUIREMENTS

- Marketing research needs (with respect to customers, marketing mix effectiveness, external environment, etc.

- Secondary data and primary data needs

- Marketing information system needs

PRODUCT

- Product class (type of consumer or business product)

- Current product life-cycle stage

- New-product development requirements (people, dollars, time, etc.)

- Product liability, safety, and social responsibility considerations

- Specification of core physical good and/or service

- Features, quality, etc.

- Supporting customer service(s) needs

- Warranty (what is covered, timing, who will support, etc.)

- Branding (Manufacture versus dealer, family brand versus individual brand, etc.)

- Packaging

- Promotion needs

- Protection needs
- Cultural sensitivity of product
- Fit with product lines

PLACE

- Objectives
- Degree of market exposure required
- Distribution customer service level required
- Type of channel (direct, indirect)
- Other channel members and/or facilitators required
- Type/number of wholesalers (agent, merchant, etc.)
- Type/number of retailers
- How discrepancies and separations will be handled
- How marketing functions are to be shared
- Coordination needed in channel
- Information requirements (EDI. Etc.)
- Transportation requirements
- Inventory requirements
- Facilities required (warehousing, distribution centers, etc.)

- Reverse channels (for returns, recalls, etc.)

PROMOTION

- Objectives
- Major message theme(s) for integrated marketing communications (desired "positioning")
- Promotion Blend
- Advertising (type, media, copy thrust, etc.)
- Personal selling (type and number of salespeople, how compensated, how effort and be allocated, etc.)
- Sales promotion (for channel members, customers, employees)

PUBLICITY

- Mix of push and pull required

PRICE

- Nature of demand (price sensitivity, elasticity)
- Demand and cost analysis
- Markup chain in channels
- Price flexibility
- Price level(s) (under what conditions)
- Adjustments to list price (geographic terms, discounts, allowances, etc.)

SPECIAL IMPLEMENTATION PROBLEMS TO BE OVERCOME

- People required

- Other resources required

CONTROL

- Marketing information system needs

- Criterion measures comparison with objectives (customer satisfaction, sales, cost, performance analysis, etc.)

FORECASTS AND ESTIMATES

- Costs (all elements in plan, over time)

- Sales (by market, over time, etc.)

- Estimated operating statement (pro forma)

TIMING

- Specific sequence of activities and events, etc.

- Likely changes over the product life cycle

CONCLUSION

How does a firm actually select a foreign market?

Well, by now you should see that the process can be logical and transparent. Hopefully, you've taken the time to go through the toolkit, listen to the audio, read the articles and white papers and explore the additional resources. You may have even given the Market Access Screen a few trial runs.

The toolkit doesn't choose a market for you and it doesn't tell you the best way to enter a chosen market. But by now your firm should be able to answer the following questions:

- What is involved in selecting a foreign market?

- How do you pick one market over another?

- What are the likely obstacles my firm will encounter overseas?

- What are some good (and bad) strategies for international market entry?

- What types of vendors and expertise will my firm need to utilize?

- What assumptions am I bringing to the table and how do I overcome them?

- Why are so many firms unsuccessful overseas and how can my company avoid failure?

- How can I "get smart" on a country?

and much, much more.

Perhaps the best compliment I can receive is an email telling me "you left something out" or "there are more issues than you mentioned." It proves that you gave the Market Entry Toolkit your attention.

And hopefully, the spirit of the audio and video reminds you that International Market Entry is not only profitable, but also fascinating.

There is nothing wrong with having many unanswered questions....I've been helping firms enter and succeed in foreign markets for years. Nobody has all of the answers.

Drop us a line to let us know how we can improve the toolkit. Or contact us if you need some expert advice.

Enjoy the journey,

Bill Decker

www.partnersinternational.com

info@partnersinternational.com

ADDITIONAL RESOURCES

No one expected this to be the end of your training and education. Now that you are familiar with global market entry, you have learned how to make good decisions. Fortunately, there are many more resources at your disposal.

THE MARKET ACCESS SCREEN:

To download and use the market access screen, please visit

www.marketaccessscreen.com

WEBSITE:

http://www.partnersinternational.com. This is the website for my firm and will contain contact information, articles, links and many other tools.

PODCAST:

http://www.internationaltoolkit.com. These free podcasts are entertaining and informative and discuss various areas of International Business.

BLOG:

http://www.lessonsfromtheroad.com. This is a free blog with articles that are updated regularly.

RADIO SHOW:

www.lemonaderadio.com. You will find this show packed with useful information on international as well as domestic business. We sprinkled in some humor to improve the taste.

VIDEO:

www.internationalbusinessminute.com. This site offers several free 1-minute videos on international business and offers a lifetime subscription to all the videos for $29.99

Please visit us on the Web

Please visit our partner sites for valuable international business tools

www.partnersinternational.com

www.internationalbusinessminute.com

www.lessonsfromtheroad.com

ADDITIONAL COPIES OF
THE MARKET ACCESS SCREEN

THE MARKET ACCESS SCREEN

Audio for this section is at <u>marketentrytoolkit.com</u>. Click on "Readers."

			Weight	Raw Score (-5 to +5)	Total	Country A
Criteria			**Weight**	**Raw Score (-5 to +5)**	**Total**	
Market Questions						
Market size			3			
Expressed market need			3			
Contacts (do you have them)			10			
Approachability (getting to the M.A.N.)			2			
Anticipated success for high margin			2			

Criteria			**Weight**	**Raw Score (-5 to +5)**	**Total**
Cultural Questions					
(Understanding theirs. More need lower #)	religious background		2		
	local language needed?		2		
	mgmt styles compatible		2		
(Longer term orientation, lower the #)	time		2		

Criteria		Weight	Raw Score (-5 to +5)	Total
Lower # if rtsp needed; don't have it)	task/ relationship	2		
(The more collective, lower the #)	individual/ collective	1		
(More context oriented, lower #)	context culture h/l	1		

Criteria		Weight	Raw Score (-5 to +5)	Total
Market environment questions				
Political understanding necessary?	(more need, lower #)	2		
Current market presence		3		
Us blocked from selling to them	(the more, the lower the #)	deal killer?		
Anti us sentiment		3		
Competitive questions				
	"taken/ available" market	3		
	5w's answerable	3		
(if there is, lower #)	strong/required local player	2		
	competitive analysis ability	3		
(No p risk is 5)	political risk	2		
Amount/infrastructure you invest		2		

Criteria		Weight	Raw Score (-5 to +5)	Total
Availability of supplier services		2		
Availability of incidental services		2		
Transparency	culture			
	business	1		
	legal	2		
	what do they regard as truth	2		
	culture	1		
(Do you know what...)	business			

Criteria		Weight	Raw Score (-5 to +5)	Total
Client questions		2		
Offset requirements (if low positive number)		3		
Do they have money?		2		
Are they a good credit risk?		2		
Ethical match				
Buying habits		2		
(Do you understand)	decision processes	2		
(Do you know)	client concerns	2		
(Do you know)	need	3		
(Do you know)	motivations	2		
Access to our firm (easy to get to us)		1		

Criteria		Weight	Raw Score (-5 to +5)	Total
Legal battlefield (is it a?)		3		
Will they need special terms?		1		
Leverage to other opportunities		2		
	in country	1		
	out of country	2		

Criteria		Weight	Raw Score (-5 to +5)	Total
Operational costs				
(High invest is neg. Number)	inward investment	3		
(More localization more negative)	product localization	1		
Local representation		1		
Legal restrictions				
(If process easy, positive #)	licenses/ permits	2		
(If process easy, positive #)	imports	3		
(Less required, higher #)	% local labor	2		
(Difficulty, more difficult is neg)	labor laws	3		
(The more needed, the lower #)	local content in product	2		

Criteria		Weight	Raw Score (-5 to +5)	Total
Modification questions				
(Less modifying, higher number)	product	3		
(Less modifying, higher number)	service	3		
Marketing				
(Less change, higher number)	how	3		
	materials	2		
(Less modifying, higher number)	delivery	2		
(Less modifying, higher number)	translation	2		
Sales				
(Less change, higher number)	methods	2		
(Shorter term, higher number)	time	2		

Criteria		Weight	Raw Score (-5 to +5)	Total
Cost of Sale				
(your cost to sell, high is lower #)				
Assuming no direct client history, not bound to certain clients, competitive product	operations (transaction)	3		
Neg 3 worst case, 3 best case, 0 neutral/don't know		3		

THE MARKET ACCESS SCREEN

Audio for this section is at <u>marketentrytoolkit.com</u>. Click on "Readers."

Criteria		Weight	Raw Score (-5 to +5)	Total
				Country A
Market Questions				
Market size		3		
Expressed market need		3		
Contacts (do you have them)		10		
Approachability (getting to the M.A.N.)		2		
Anticipated success for high margin		2		

Criteria		Weight	Raw Score (-5 to +5)	Total
Cultural Questions				
(Understanding theirs. More need lower #)	religious background	2		
	local language needed?	2		
	mgmt styles compatible	2		
(Longer term orientation, lower the #)	time	2		

Criteria		Weight	Raw Score (-5 to +5)	Total
Lower # if rtsp needed; don't have it)	task/ relationship	2		
(The more collective, lower the #)	individual/ collective	1		
(More context oriented, lower #)	context culture h/l	1		

Criteria		Weight	Raw Score (-5 to +5)	Total
Market environment questions				
Political understanding necessary?	(more need, lower #)	2		
Current market presence		3		
Us blocked from selling to them	(the more, the lower the #)	deal killer?		
Anti us sentiment		3		
Competitive questions				
	"taken/ available" market	3		
	5w's answerable	3		
(if there is, lower #)	strong/required local player	2		
	competitive analysis ability	3		
(No p risk is 5)	political risk	2		
Amount/infrastructure you invest		2		

Criteria		Weight	Raw Score (-5 to +5)	Total
Availability of supplier services		2		
Availability of incidental services		2		
Transparency	culture			
	business	1		
	legal	2		
	what do they regard as truth	2		
	culture	1		
(Do you know what...)	business			

Criteria		Weight	Raw Score (-5 to +5)	Total
Client questions		**2**		
Offset requirements (if low positive number)		3		
Do they have money?		2		
Are they a good credit risk?		2		
Ethical match				
Buying habits		2		
(Do you understand)	decision processes	2		
(Do you know)	client concerns	2		
(Do you know)	need	3		
(Do you know)	motivations	2		
Access to our firm (easy to get to us)		1		

Criteria		Weight	Raw Score (-5 to +5)	Total
Legal battlefield (is it a?)		3		
Will they need special terms?		1		
Leverage to other opportunities		2		
	in country	1		
	out of country	2		

Criteria		Weight	Raw Score (-5 to +5)	Total
Operational costs				
(High invest is neg. Number)	inward investment	3		
(More localization more negative)	product localization	1		
Local representation		1		
Legal restrictions				
(If process easy, positive #)	licenses/permits	2		
(If process easy, positive #)	imports	3		
(Less required, higher #)	% local labor	2		
(Difficulty, more difficult is neg)	labor laws	3		
(The more needed, the lower #)	local content in product	2		

184

Criteria		Weight	Raw Score (-5 to +5)	Total
Modification questions				
(Less modifying, higher number)	product	3		
(Less modifying, higher number)	service	3		
Marketing				
(Less change, higher number)	how	3		
	materials	2		
(Less modifying, higher number)	delivery	2		
(Less modifying, higher number)	translation	2		
Sales				
(Less change, higher number)	methods	2		
(Shorter term, higher number)	time	2		

Criteria		Weight	Raw Score (-5 to +5)	Total
Cost of Sale				
(your cost to sell, high is lower #)				
Assuming no direct client history, not bound to certain clients, competitive product	operations (transaction)	3		
Neg 3 worst case, 3 best case, 0 neutral/don't know		3		

THE MARKET ACCESS SCREEN

Audio for this section is at <u>marketentrytoolkit.com</u>. Click on "Readers."

Criteria		Weight	Raw Score (-5 to +5)	Total
				Country A
Market Questions				
Market size		3		
Expressed market need		3		
Contacts (do you have them)		10		
Approachability (getting to the M.A.N.)		2		
Anticipated success for high margin		2		

Criteria		Weight	Raw Score (-5 to +5)	Total
Cultural Questions				
(Understanding theirs. More need lower #)	religious background	2		
	local language needed?	2		
	mgmt styles compatible	2		
(Longer term orientation, lower the #)	time	2		

Criteria		Weight	Raw Score (-5 to +5)	Total
Lower # if rtsp needed; don't have it)	task/ relationship	2		
(The more collective, lower the #)	individual/ collective	1		
(More context oriented, lower #)	context culture h/l	1		

Criteria		Weight	Raw Score (-5 to +5)	Total
Market environment questions				
Political understanding necessary?	(more need, lower #)	2		
Current market presence		3		
Us blocked from selling to them	(the more, the lower the #)	deal killer?		
Anti us sentiment		3		
Competitive questions				
	"taken/ available" market	3		
	5w's answerable	3		
(if there is, lower #)	strong/required local player	2		
	competitive analysis ability	3		
(No p risk is 5)	political risk	2		
Amount/infrastructure you invest		2		

Criteria		Weight	Raw Score (-5 to +5)	Total
Availability of supplier services		2		
Availability of incidental services		2		
Transparency	culture			
	business	1		
	legal	2		
	what do they regard as truth	2		
	culture	1		
(Do you know what...)	business			

Criteria		Weight	Raw Score (-5 to +5)	Total
Client questions		**2**		
Offset requirements (if low positive number)		3		
Do they have money?		2		
Are they a good credit risk?		2		
Ethical match				
Buying habits		2		
(Do you understand)	decision processes	2		
(Do you know)	client concerns	2		
(Do you know)	need	3		
(Do you know)	motivations	2		
Access to our firm (easy to get to us)		1		

Criteria		Weight	Raw Score (-5 to +5)	Total
Legal battlefield (is it a?)		3		
Will they need special terms?		1		
Leverage to other opportunities		2		
	in country	1		
	out of country	2		

Criteria		Weight	Raw Score (-5 to +5)	Total
Operational costs				
(High invest is neg. Number)	inward investment	3		
(More localization more negative)	product localization	1		
Local representation		1		
Legal restrictions				
(If process easy, positive #)	licenses/ permits	2		
(If process easy, positive #)	imports	3		
(Less required, higher #)	% local labor	2		
(Difficulty, more difficult is neg)	labor laws	3		
(The more needed, the lower #)	local content in product	2		

Criteria		Weight	Raw Score (-5 to +5)	Total
Modification questions				
(Less modifying, higher number)	product	3		
(Less modifying, higher number)	service	3		
Marketing				
(Less change, higher number)	how	3		
	materials	2		
(Less modifying, higher number)	delivery	2		
(Less modifying, higher number)	translation	2		
Sales				
(Less change, higher number)	methods	2		
(Shorter term, higher number)	time	2		

Criteria		Weight	Raw Score (-5 to +5)	Total
Cost of Sale				
(your cost to sell, high is lower #)				
Assuming no direct client history, not bound to certain clients, competitive product	operations (transaction)	3		
Neg 3 worst case, 3 best case, 0 neutral/don't know		3		

18972673R00108

Made in the USA
San Bernardino, CA
07 February 2015